Parenting Adhd

A Different Perspective on Parenting

(A Practical Guide to Building Cooperation and Connecting With Your Child)

Jonathan Bell

Published by Rob Miles

© **Jonathan Bell**

All Rights Reserved

Parenting Adhd: A Different Perspective on Parenting (A Practical Guide to Building Cooperation and Connecting With Your Child)

ISBN 9781990084461

All rights reserved. No part of this guide may be reproduced in any form without permission in writing from the publisher except in the case of brief quotations embodied in critical articles or reviews.

Legal & Disclaimer

The information contained in this book is not designed to replace or take the place of any form of medicine or professional medical advice. The information in this book has been provided for educational and entertainment purposes only.

The information contained in this book has been compiled from sources deemed reliable, and it is accurate to the best of the Author's knowledge; however, the Author cannot guarantee its accuracy and validity and cannot be held liable for any errors or omissions. Changes are periodically made to this book. You must consult your doctor or get professional medical advice before using any of the suggested remedies, techniques, or information in this book.

Upon using the information contained in this book, you agree to hold harmless the Author from and against any damages, costs, and expenses, including any legal fees potentially resulting from the application of any of the information provided by this guide. This disclaimer applies to any damages or injury caused by the use and application, whether directly or indirectly, of any advice or information presented, whether for breach of contract, tort, negligence, personal injury, criminal intent, or under any other cause of action.

You agree to accept all risks of using the information presented inside this book. You need to consult a professional medical practitioner in order to ensure you are both able and healthy enough to participate in this program.

Table of Contents

INTRODUCTION 1

CHAPTER 1: CHECK YOUR EXPECTATIONS 3

CHAPTER 2: THOSE WHO DON'T 11

CHAPTER 3: WHAT CAN YOU EXPECT? 19

CHAPTER 4: FAMILY GATHERINGS 25

CHAPTER 5: ACKNOWLEDGE 31

CHAPTER 6: WHEN AND HOW TO START DISCIPLINE 40

CHAPTER 7 49

CHAPTER 8: HOW THE CHALLENGE OF SINGLE PARENTING AFFECTS YOUR DECISION TO DIVORCE 54

CHAPTER 9: CO-PARENTING FOR TWO 60

CHAPTER 10: PLANNING TO GO SOLO 69

CHAPTER 11: RULES OF THUMB-LENGTH OF TIME 73

CHAPTER 12: WHEN & WHY OUR WORDS MATTER 82

CHAPTER 13: UNLEASHING YOUR CHILD'S IMAGINATIVE AND CREATIVE POWER 98

CHAPTER 14: TODDLER PROOFING 107

CHAPTER 15: CAUSES OF PARENTING PITFALLS 112

CHAPTER 16: PEOPLE CONSIDERING HAVING CHILDREN 118

CHAPTER 17: HOW TO STOP A BITING CHILD 122

CHAPTER 18: SETTING A SCHEDULE FOR YOUR TODDLER 131

CHAPTER 19: THE IMPORTANCE OF GOOD NUTRITION: WHAT FOODS SHOULD YOU FEED YOUR CHILD 135

CHAPTER 20: HOW DIVORCE AFFECTS YOUR CHILDREN 144

CHAPTER 21: A PHYSICAL EPIDEMIC AMONG KIDS 151

CHAPTER 22: CHILD SUPPORT AFTER DIVORCE 155

CHAPTER 23: THE NEED FOR UNDERSTANDING NUTRITIONAL LABELS IN A WORLD OF TOXIC INGREDIENTS 159

CHAPTER 24: COPING WHEN THINGS GO WRONG 165

CHAPTER 25: DEVELOPMENTAL CONSIDERATIONS 171

CHAPTER 26: SKIN PROTECTION WITH KIDS 179

CHAPTER 27: FOOD FOR THOUGHT 186

CHAPTER 28: YOUR CHILD NEEDS TO PLAY AND HAVE A HOBBY 194

CHAPTER 29: PARENTING PLANS 199

CONCLUSION 202

Introduction

Parenting is the most challenging job that anyone will face in his or her lives.It could be so much easier for parents if their children were easier to handle.However, when their kids are rather stubborn, parents will need some techniques on how to handle them in a way that can result to a better understanding between them and their child.

In this book, I have tried to convey the point of view of both parents and children and have come up with some very valuable suggestions.These suggestions could help parents handle their children who may be uncontrollable and difficult to deal with. Let's face it, it is tough to struggle with which seems to be something that is uncontrollable (your child) but we as parents need to practice some very hard in the moment, patience calmness and sense in an storm of emotions in the moment of crisis. We need to be that ROCK for our child. The calm in their struggles, they are changing and the world is going so fast, we need to be there for them!! I Truly Hope that this book will bring you the calmness and the composer you need for YOUR child.

With this new sense of composer, you will gain trust with your child, and an understanding and open up the communication between You and Your Child like never before.

I wish you the best in life that is why I write these books so we ALL may live happier and healthier. To open communication for that is the ONLY way problems can be eliminated. To open communication one must establish trust and to establish trust one must listen!! It is a give and take by both sides.

Thanks again for downloading this book. I hope you enjoy it!

Chapter 1: Check Your Expectations

The first and possibly most important thing for any soon to be parent to realize is that you are not ready and you never will be. I don't care how many books, blogs and studies you have read or how many great parents, doctors, and child psychologists you have interviewed before the birth of your child. You are not ready.

Now, don't let that scare you. Well, it can scare you a bit. A little fear in the face of the awesome responsibility of parenthood is a good and healthy thing. The fact that no one is really ready, and yet we have been doing it for many, many centuries and millennia by now shows that we are also pretty good at making it up as we go along.

Almost every person is hard-wired to be a parent and all of those in-born instincts will come to the surface and help you get through those tough first few weeks.Still, it will wind up testing you in unexpected ways.

And even the things you do expect like sleepless nights, dirty diapers, projectile vomit, and more, the actual experience is different than what you picture in your head.

Now, I don't want to scare you off here.Being a parent is awesome, but it is awesome in a way that is difficult to explain.Even as I type this, there is a deep seated joy in my soul at the thought of being a parent.There are no words to convey it.

And yet, it is important to acknowledge that the joy I speak of comes with a lot of work and responsibility.Too many people will only talk about the great things without acknowledging how demanding the task of parenting can be.

If that is all a person hears, then after the third night of two-hour's sleep and sticking your hand straight into the weird yellow goo that has filled the diaper, he could be forgiven for thinking he had been made a fool of.

So, all of that said, what should you expect?

The first two to four weeks with your first child will likely be the hardest of your life.I distinctly remember thinking around two weeks in that I might never shower or eat a cooked meal ever again.

Fortunately there were friends and family who helped out by bringing lots of prepared food over. The point is that children, especially babies tend to cry and as a first-time parent, you are going to want to find the problem and solve it as quickly as possible.It is simply human nature to be protective of your first child.

As that first little bundle of joy becomes an ever larger bundle and learns to craw and then walk.When that happens, I hope you already have locks installed on your cupboard doors.Children are curious, especially about whatever might be hiding under all the pots and pans and they will throw them all over the kitchen to find out.

Also, don't think that you can safely set a cup of coffee (your new best friend) on an end table for the next few years.My children have all gone through a phase where they could not abide anything being set on a flat surface.Unless that flat surface is the floor.Everything belongs on the floor.

And of course there are the things that no one could predict.My first child had some trouble nursing so we had to bring her to the hospital just a couple days after leaving to have her weighed.For the sake of accuracy, we had to weigh her naked.

While transferring her from the changing table to the scale, she decided it was the perfect time to empty her tiny bowels all over my white t-shirt.Well, only a fairly small oval on the shirt.

Fortunately, I had taken my own advice and so was not terribly surprised at something random like that happening.And my wife, the doc, and I were able to have a laugh over it.

That is going to be one of the single biggest factors to being a good parent, having a sense of humor.If you can't laugh at yourself, at your kids and the crazy things you all do, it's going to be a rough road.Just remember that nothing any of you have done is new.

Lots of parents have gotten pooped on, kids will always empty your purse all over the floor (including any embarrassing contents and probably in front of friends or family), and at least one will find a favorite colorful expletive that they will shout at the top of their lungs in the store.

Don't worry.Those people laughing at you are probably laughing because they have had the same things happen to them.Best to laugh along.

As for social life, that will take a back seat for a while. There just isn't going to be time for that. Even if you are fortunate enough to live near some grandparents, even the most willing are not going to want to babysit every weekend.

You aren't going to make the hockey game every week or see every movie on opening weekend, or go out dancing very often.

For the most part, this is hardest to adjust too with the first child. After all, only one child is still one that needs to be taken care of. And contrary to popular belief, this is harder the older you are when you have that first child. The longer you go without having one, the more set in your ways you become and the bigger culture shock parenthood will be.

Once you accept the fact that you don't get to be the life of every party anymore and focus on just being a good parent, this won't bother you much. And it won't even be an issue once you have more children.

I honestly think that many parents have very few children because they think that every child will be just as much of a life style altering experience.The truth is that it isn't.Once you get the hang of taking care of one, a second is really just a little bit more of what you are already used to.

Now, I think after all of that I need to repeat that I don't want to scare you off.I just want you to know that it isn't all going to be sunshine and rainbows.But there are a lot of those too.

Particularly when you have more than one child.One of the greatest gifts you can give your child is a brother or sister.And trust me, while you will need to play referee from time to time, there is no denying how great it is to watch them grow together.

There is a great deal of joy in watching your child grow and discover the world.A simple giggle during a piggy-back ride or wide-eyed look of awe at some new toy, or even the first touch of grass is worth a thousand diaper changes.

And what I usually say in reply to those who talk about how much work it is and how much you lose is that no TV, car, hockey game, or dancing lesson will every run to me and hug me when I come home from work.

Only a child will do that.Only a child will look at you with perfectly innocent eyes and say, "I love you."

Chapter 2: Those Who Don't

I know.I know.This is a rather odd way to begin a book that portends to be good advice.For as the old adage goes, "those who know how, do, and those who don't, teach."That is not to say that you should refrain from the counsel of others.On the contrary, when my friends come to me to inquire about anything that matters, I always encourage them to not end with my counsel alone, but to seek the advice of others as well.And there in, lies the point.**It is the abundance of counsel that supplies the thread of wisdom.**

But advice, in our western culture, has become like ice cream: there is always a flavor of the day.That approach has made billions of dollars in our overactive diet industry.Every year yields scores of new 'guaranteed ways' to get your body to look like that little plastic Mattel doll every woman seems to loathe.And men are no longer immune to the insanity.Don't eat carbs.Eat only carbs.Take this pill.Eat more Star Fruit.We buy book, after book, after book, after book.And the results are annoyingly predictable: we are rapidly becoming the most obese generation in the history of the planet.In other words, we are obsessed with 'those who don't,' and the so-called experts of the diet industry are making millions off our misery.

That brings us to my friend Bob.His mother could have been accused of being a card-carrying member of the disciples of the expert of her day.In fact, she followed that expert's advice to the letter.This expert had a revolutionary idea back in the 1960s: puree any food you choose and feed it to your baby.The result was rather predictable.Bob, as a grown man, is allergic to his own edible shadow.You might say he's a real meat and potatoes guy- but not by choice.His mother followed the advice of the 'expert of the day-' and only the expert of the day.Consequently, her child has paid for it ever since.

'Those who don't...'

Scientists love their laboratories and clinical environments.They love rats in mazes.They love beakers and test tubes and cages.They love not just the experiment, but the ability to control the environment the experiment takes place in as well.For instance, in drug testing, there is always a control group: a separate group of people, as close to identical to the test group as possible, not given whatever drug they are testing.There is nothing wrong with this line of thinking.It is necessary to effectively test many important hypothesis.Such thinking has helped us understand many things we previously did not.

However, anyone who has ever lived in a family knows that it bares no resemblance to a clinical or laboratory environment.Chaos reigns- at times- even in the best of families.The family is a plethora of free wills attempting to be contained within a liquid structure.In fact, to reproduce something similar to the family environment in a laboratory, a scientist would have to attempt to mix a safe chemical concoction while two other scientists maliciously tried to add drops of other chemicals to the beaker guaranteed to create an unstable, volatile, substance.This would all take place while a 35,ooo watt sound system produced so much bass thump that all of the beakers, droppers and test tubes involved would bounce like Tigger through the Hundred Acre Wood.No scientist, in his right mind, would ever work under these conditions.That is, of course, unless that scientist enters the jungles of parenting in his or her personal life.

Therefore, there is no scientific psychological experiment that can ever properly simulate anything close to the reality known as family.Each family is its own experiment.No two dads are exactly alike.No two moms are exactly alike.No two parents relate to each other in exactly the same way.Without adding a single child to this mix we are in a position where a single postulate may prove more often ineffective, than effective.

That is not to say that all things said by experts are invalid.On the contrary, many 'experts' have offered counsel that can prove key to the parenting process.**The problem is not with them, the problem is with us**.Let me say it again: we Americans tend to gravitate to singular sources (flavors of the day).Parenting is a potluck, not a one-course meal.Potlucks are best when you invite all of the best cooks in your circle of influence.In parenting, not all the 'best cooks' make their living handing out their recipes for success.Just like in cooking, many of the 'best cooks' cook only at home.

Parenting is best when we understand, 'The Power in The Plural.'We would all love to invite Rachel Ray or Gordon Ramsey or some other celebrity cook to our potluck.But if all we had to eat at the potluck is what one of them brought, the meal would be lacking both the quantity and the variety that make a potluck such an enjoyable experience.However, if that potluck had one of their dishes in addition to Grandpa's chili, Aunt Martha's Peach Jell-O, Uncle Tom's Slow Smoked Ribs and Mother's Apple Pie, everyone, including our celebrity cooks, would find a plurality of flavors to put smiles on their faces.

As parents, we need to understand that **parenting requires a buffet line of advice** in order to find the very things that will best motivate our children to become the type of people we hope they will be.We need 'experts,' but we need to understand that they do not always come with Ivy League Degrees on their walls.There is a whole generation of people who have successfully parented (you turned okay, didn't you?Okay, maybe not.).They have lots of ideas about raising children; and some of them are actually good (truthfully, many of them are).Even if your parents failed you, there are others around you (relatives, neighbors, co-workers, parents of your adult friends) who can offer counsel that will prove useful to you in the parenting process.

Beyond our elders, there are also those who parent along side you. Your children have friends who have parents as well (apologies for overstating the obvious). If the child proves to be well behaved, it just might behoove you to ask why. Becoming friends with the parents of your children's friends will lead to what we will talk about in the next chapter. But it will also lead to the opportunities to share both successes and failures. That means you can take short cuts to successful parenting by learning from the failures (or successes) other parents have already made. Such conversations are a win-win as everyone benefits, especially the children. The only thing that might stand in your way is your own pride.

Finally, be especially careful of 'those who don't.' Taking advice from people who have never raised children of their own is like military generals getting advice on military strategy from comic books.Single friends might accidentally give you the right advice, but would you not rather have advice that comes from practical, real world experience?We, likewise, should be careful with advise from counselors (even those within the psychological or religious communities) who do not have children of their own.The reality is that the advice they dispense is nothing more then a regurgitation of a book they have read or a professor they have listened to.Now that book (or professor) may have some extraordinary advice, but you are getting that advice second hand (ever played telephone?).Again, I am not saying to not take their advice.But be wise and seek other counsel as well.Wisdom, especially in parenting, requires the counsel of many, filtered through what

you already know to be wise.

Chapter 3: What Can You Expect?

What is the secret of those parents who raised extraordinarily successful children, starting from their earliest years? One thing is for sure, they had to do something extraordinary. After all, usually, we raise "well-behaved" children. We take them to the zoo, enroll them in kindergarten, and then in school. And it's rare that those children are later extraordinarily successful. In the biographies of outstanding individuals it is noticeable that, indeed, their parents did extraordinary things in their children's childhood. However, it wasn't anything as marvelous or incredible as you might expect.

Those outstanding individuals' parents would allow them to experience and make plenty of mistakes, and put their ideas (even the odd ones) into practice. Unfortunately, in our culture, we are discouraged from odd ideas, punished for mistakes, and afraid of new experiences. Therefore, although it may seem inconspicuous, strong will is required both from parents and their children.

Yet, there is good news. You're not an ordinary parent (who only wants their child to be good and raised without any greater effort)!Believe me, I know my clients, and the ordinary parents NEVER have chosen books entitled "Entrepreneurial child". Moreover, these "ordinary" parents have often blamed me for being negative about the school system :)

You, on the other hand, are a parent who cares about your child's development. I assume that you are the kind of a parent who has noticed some flaws in the system we've been living in. No matter whether it's about the education or political system - both are extremely flawed. I also assume, that you're the parent who has chosen this book for a reason. Perhaps you've already been raising an entrepreneurial child and you are curious what techniques have been used by others. Perhaps you've been using some alternative child-raising methods and you're curious about the new concept of entrepreneurship.

Or, perhaps you're slightly suspicious about this e-book. You're not convinced enough that teaching such little children "adult" matters may have any sense. Well, I can respond to any of the above mentioned issues.

This e-book deals with two most important aspects inevitable in raising children, successful in their future lives. These aspects are: financial education and personal development. Their importance will be explained in the first chapter. The term and the whole concept of "an entrepreneurial child" (secrets of which you'll learn in a bit) have originated from a combination of financial education and personal development of children.

One thing is for sure, you can't learn how to be entrepreneurial in school, as well as you can't learn it from children's cartoons. So if you want to raise a resourceful, self-reliant and confident child, you need to rely on yourself. Because either you will be the one who forms the character of your child, or the environment will do it for you. I present you 10 chapters which will teach you how to raise an entrepreneurial child and why it is so important.

The following issues will be discussed:

1. What is the reason for teaching children entrepreneurship?

2. How do you know if your child is predisposed to be entrepreneurial? Are they capable of it?

3. Goals, successes and failures - teach your child how to cope with them.

4. Financial literacy. What should you teach your child?

5. Inevitable leadership skills that you can instill in your child.

6. Different characters make different entrepreneurs.

7. Creating savings and motivational goals.

8. A young, skillful investor.

9. What entrepreneurial activities can be undertaken by a child - a collection of ideas.

10. Examples of young entrepreneurs + VIDEOS.

Never in the history have children had so plenty of opportunities to create their own future. And never have parents had so plenty of strategies of motivating their children to develop and perfect their minds or characters. Knowledge is at your fingertips!

It's not easy to be a child. Adults have a tendency to teach their children to be quiet at school, memorize facts, and get good grades. They also often tell them not to work and make mistakes. So how are the children raised in this way supposed to participate in social life? Where are they to learn the rules of a complicated world of mundane challenges?

However, there are many bold, alert and confident children who push forward, do incredible things, win awards. They're never bored and can always find something to do. Not only do they talk to their parents, but also work with them. As we can tell from history, these children will make discoveries, make dreams come true, achieve fame, get to the top, and enrich the world, making it a great place to live in.

Finally, there are several assumptions I've made:

- children can think for themselves at an early age;

- fair trade ethics is a better way of getting self-respect than social theories that teach self-sacrifice and obedience to authorities;

- doing useful things at a young age is as good for young poets and scientists as for young entrepreneurs;

And now you've learned the basics and the purpose of this e-book. Enjoy your reading!

Chapter 4: Family Gatherings

The first rule of the house is that all children must sit down with the family for their breakfast and their evening meal. It doesn't matter what age the child is. This rule should be made clear because it helps everyone. This is a time when things can be discussed. I was always encouraged as a child to be quiet during eating times and I remember feeling a resentment because of that rule. What happened in my case was that my parents and my siblings rarely got together to talk about anything. We were either sitting together at the meal table in silence, or we were expected to sit in front of the TV mindlessly watching programs that were approved of by my parents.

Family gatherings open up opportunities for several things and I believe the best place for you all to gather for these meals is around the kitchen table. You need everyone to participate. Kids can lay the table. Older kids can help in the preparation of the food. If a kid is inclined to enjoy cooking, encourage it. At the meal table, you need to sit at the head of the table. I find that having the head of the table seat gives you a little authority without making you look like a dictator. It also allows you to serve the food comfortably. If you also have a calendar for the family, this should always be close at hand so that you can go around the different members of the family and use the calendar for these reasons:

Firm up dates that are important to the kids

Make sure that you are aware of their medical appointments

Make sure that you know what deadlines your kids have

Make plans for things that you can do together that are fun

What you are using is something called habit stacking. The habit is that you all sit down together and the new habit is using the event to make sure that all of your appointments and obligations are met. You are also able to discuss with kids whether there is anything that they would like to do at the weekend as a family event. Kids come up with all sorts of ideas and they are not all expensive. If you worry about money, then you need to come up with creative ideas and if you give the kids a challenge at breakfast, you can be sure that they will come up with solutions by the evening meal. Let me show you an example.

Children enjoy being challenged and having their mental energy put into something where there is some sort of reward at the end. Thus you can challenge them:

This weekend, we need a plan. Something we can all do together that doesn't cost a lot but that involves nature and art.

This weekend, we want to go and visit something interesting locally. Come up with an idea of something that will be fun for everyone and reasons why you think your idea is a good one.

What you are doing is involving the kids and that's very important from an early age. You may have plans to do a project in the garden and you can come up with ideas they will enjoy in the same way, using the breakfast to sow the seeds of ideas and the evening meal to make firm plans. To make sure they are listening, no cell phones are permitted at the table. Kids should be taught to be respectful and you need to set the example. If you always have your cell phone switched on, make a point of switching yours off before you ask them to do likewise. That way, they can hardly grumble that you are being unreasonable.

You also need to make sure that your kids know all of their relatives. Even if someone irritates you, an aunt with a car can be a very useful ally, when you are stuck for transport and if the aunt is particularly keen on the kids, you get less resistance. Encourage your relatives to come to tea sometimes and having a barbecue for all of your family on a hot summer's day can give you the chance to get help whenever you need it. There has to be something in it for those that help you and if friendship and closeness is there, then it will be easier to enlist the help of those family members. If you think that it would work better to offer money for gas for the car, then this is a potential thing to suggest so that your relatives don't feel put upon. Similarly, when you have kids, your mom and dad become very strong allies to have and can always help out during school vacation times when you cannot give the kids the hours that you feel you should.

A lot of parents make the mistake of leaving things up until the last minute and then insisting that grandparents take the kids. This doesn't help because it causes the kids to resent being sent to grandma's house all the time and grandma soon gets fed up of being used. However, when you create a give and take situation where relatives are constantly involved in your kids' lives, that's a whole new ballgame.

Chapter 5: Acknowledge

.Spend just a few minutes writing a note to yourself. All the things you wish you could say to someone. The things you might keep hidden because you don't want to complain, or you don't want anyone to know you're struggling with. This is just for you, so be honest.Write in the first person. Here are some prompts if you need them:

Dear Me,

I want you to know…

These last few days/weeks/months have been…

You have handled them with ….

But I want you to know that I've seen…. Identify Your Hardship

This might sound really obvious, but it's important to identify your hardship. By the time you're feeling overwhelmed enough to pick up a book like this, there's probably more than one single thing going on in your life. Or maybe there is just one thing, but it's so big you don't know where to start.

Identifying your feelings can help you explain your reactions. For example, if your child spills water all over the floor and you just flip out and yell and totally overreact, you know in your heart of hearts that a little spilled water isn't really the issue. So what **is** the issue? The fact that you feel unheard? Unappreciated? With everything else you've got going on, the fact that you now have to mop a floor too?

When you can answer that, you can start to find ways to fix it. In that example the answer might be that you need to all go for a walk, or do something fun. Or it could simply be that you're really in need of a break. By identifying the feeling, you also take responsibility for it, and you are able to change the direction of your thoughts and actions for the rest of the day.

But how on earth do I separate all the things that are causing me this overwhelm?

For example: my marriage is over, I feel stressed every time I look around my house and my kids haven't seen me smile in months and every time I walk into the kitchen I want to cry for all the laundry and dishes piled up everywhere.

Activity 2: Identify

Write down all the things that worry you, that make you feel miserable when you walk into your home, or that make you feel like life is hard. There are no right or wrong answers. Be honest with yourself.

Categorise Your Hardship

Now that you've acknowledged that things are hard, and identified what the hardships are, it's time to categorise them.

When you look at all the problems as one big lump, it is overwhelming. It's like a mountain of laundry. By emptying the laundry tub out in the living room and taking one item at a time to the appropriate wardrobe, you will eventually get through the pile, but it will take all day and you'll be exhausted from running up and down. Instead you might categorise it into type: here are all the socks, here are all the pants, here are all the shirts. And then you might categorise it into person. These are all John's socks. There are all Sarah's socks. And once you've separated all the laundry into categories, you can quickly put everything in its place.

You can deal with your hardships the same way.

By identifying what the problem is you can break it down, and begin to confront it.

Some problems are obvious. **My mother just died. My husband just left me. I lost my job**. These are the life-altering problems we all face at some point. They are huge, and have the opportunity to change the direction of our futures. They also are likely to take the longest to 'deal' with.

Some problems are long-term problems. These are ones that are going to take time and determination, but chances are that you can fix them. Things like debt, joblessness, even some critical illnesses. Their fixability doesn't make them any less painful when you're facing it. Not having money to send your child on a field trip all their friends are going on hurts. It can make you short-tempered and tetchy. But it is, usually, solvable.

Other problems are circumstantial or temporary. Sometimes we just have to get through them. Other times they have simple solutions. **My house is overcrowded. We have no storage space. The vacuum cleaner has stopped working.**

And sometimes, the fact that the vacuum cleaner has stopped working can be the thing that causes us to utterly melt down. We coped with the big things, we even helped other people out, but when the vacuum cleaner stopped while we were vacuuming up a pile of sand brought in from the beach, we snap. You've heard of the final straw? The one that broke the camel's back? Sometimes it's the little things, all piled up.

Many times overwhelm actually comes from the smaller things. Many little things, overrunning our minds, our schedules and our days, so many that not only do we have no time to even think of the bigger issues, but we don't get through the list of the smaller things. But the truth is, many of these 'smaller' things are immediate things that can be ticked off a list quickly and easily.

Do not ignore the quick and immediate things because they clutter up your mind, robbing you of the energy you need to deal with the big things.

I can't tell you which things to put in which category. That is entirely up to you. What I might consider a short-term problem might be a huge situation for you. A life-altering change for one person could be simply a sweet relief for another.

Here are some pointers, though: The quick fixes are things that you could realistically sort out today/this week or without making major changes. They are the small changes with big rewards (the stack of dishes you never seem to get to the end of that cause you frustration every time you walk into the kitchen. Or the craft drawer that makes you dread craft time because you can never find anything.)

Long term problems things are those that are going to take a little more planning – a new storage unit that you're going to have to save up for, a driver's licence so that you don't have to wait for the bus in the rain every day, consistent application for jobs, attending interviews, keeping at 'it', whatever 'it' may be.

Life-altering things things can be broken down too, but you can't always arrange easy fixes for them. Sometimes time is the only healer, sometimes you need a little help. But when your head has less clutter from all the 'smaller' problems, you can start working out what you need to get you through the bigger ones.

Take death, for example. No amount of planning is going to fix that. But grief counselling for an hour a week can make the world of difference.

But I don't have time?!

Actually, once you've fixed some of the smaller things that consume your emotional and mental energy, you may just be surprised to find you suddenly do have more time.

But I don't have money?!

Not having money is something I understand all too well. Again, though, if you are not living in a state of continual chaos, you may just find you can actually afford a few sessions with a grief counsellor. Or you could find a free service. Sometimes the hardest thing, in times of hardship, is finding the energy to pick up the phone. Clear your life of the smaller hardships, and you'll have so much more energy to deal with the bigger ones.

Or maybe it's not grief counselling that you need, but simply time to grieve.

Identify what you're feeling, and figure out why. Things aren't always as obvious as they look. Even with death – like pregnancy, marriage and moving – it brings up a lot of emotions, and generally not the ones you would have expected.

Chapter 6: When And How To Start

Discipline

The foundation to easy and successful discipline is established during the infancy period. The parents form a strong bond with the infant while addressing the needs. Emotional attachment is established as trust begins to develop. The key is to give consistent care in the most loving manner. Parents are encouraged to actively be involved in providing the infant's daily care. Play time is also encouraged to promote strong and healthy bond. This bond is to be nurtured all throughout the child's life.

When disciplining your child, there are a few points to consider. Each negative behavior does not warrant a punishment every time. There are instances when you need to let some behavior pass. Here are a few guidelines to consider before you start punishing or scolding your child.

1. Understand the motive of the behavior

It is easy to scold a child for every misdeed. Before doing so, take a moment to try to understand why the child is behaving that way. Sometimes, children misbehave in order to gain attention. It is easy to forget that your child needs and wants you to pay attention to them even for just a few minutes. Misbehaviors might be a desperate attempt to gain a parent's attention. It is a good idea to see the pattern of the child's behavior in relation to the parent's. Once you see a connection, reorient activities and behavior to match that of the child. Simply put, if the child becomes difficult at times when you are busy with work, try to spend more time with him before you embark on your other duties.

Parents may also fail to realize that the child is not willfully misbehaving. The child may actually be doing the best he or she can. The behavior may be an attempt to meet the parent's expectations, but was not quite able to do so. Recognize the effort, not the failure to reach the standard behavior. The first responsibility of parents is to know the reason for the behavior. Correcting it is secondary. Consider the child's developmental level. Sometimes, parents expect too much from their children. Make some allowances, especially in younger children. Recognize what they can and cannot do for their age.

According to Kathryn J. Kvols, children misbehave when they feel powerless and discouraged about a situation. Parents who spank and scold these children will make them feel even worse about themselves. It is a vicious cycle that only parents can put an end to. Hold the children up and make them feel better, and the misdeeds will be corrected by themselves. It makes no sense and is counterproductive to scold and discourage children who already feel bad about themselves.

To fully understand why the child misbehaves, consider a few factors. Identify the particular behavior. What exactly did the child do? Then consider how you feel about the behavior. Parents may feel disappointed and feel inadequate as parents. Avoid projecting these feelings to the child. Then asses the child's developmental stage, the emotions, and the needs. Know where the behavior is occurring and who are present in the setting. Misdeeds may be a reflection of the relationship the child has with the place and the people in it. Most importantly, assess the kind of relationship you have with the child. Evaluate how much quality time you spend together. Quality time means time spent bonding with the child. Do you spend time playing? Do you show genuine attention and interest to what your child is telling you? Lack of these may result to misbehavior in an attempt to catch your attention.

2. Control yourself before you control your child

Discipline is most successful if the parents model the desired behavior. Practice what you preach. Take a moment to look at your own behavior. Children might not be behaving as expected because the parent does not follow his own rule. Example, children may not want to fix the toys because they see the parent's own things strewn around the house.

Parents often lose their temper when dealing with their children's behavior. Most of the time, parents yell at their children for misbehaving. Worse, parents resort to hitting them for every undesirable behavior. Yelling is very ineffective to use with children. It will only give a negative impression on them. Before you lose your head, breathe and count to 10. Calm yourself before dealing with the child. They are more likely to listen when you talk to them in a calm manner. Yelling and hitting make them focus on the physical and emotional pain it inflicts, rather than on the message you want to tell them. If in case you do lose your temper with your child, take a break. Walk away and calm yourself. Then go back and talk to the child in a more loving manner. Reconnect and explain why you scolded him. Never forget to reassure the child of your love.

3. Be consistent

Sometimes, parents are too exhausted with the daily grind that they choose to overlook certain behaviors. They let misdeeds pass because they do not have the energy to scold their child. Sometimes, parents think that the behavior will pass. Be consistent. This is the key to discipline. Send a firm and definite message that wrong is wrong at all times.

Tell off a child when behaving inappropriately. If the child repeats the offense, remove the child from the situation. Avoid ignoring the child if the behavior is repeated or persistent. The child may be trying to test the limits. Sometimes, they will argue with the parent over the rules. Do not even attempt to go that way because no one emerges as a winner. The situation will only escalate, and hurt feelings will result. When the child starts to argue, tell the rule in a firm and resolute manner. If the child persists, tell the child that you love him and that you will not argue with him over the issue anymore.

In case an argument is inevitable, make sure that everyone leaves with their dignities intact. Avoid using harsh words and belittling the child. Treat them the way you want to be treated- with respect. Consider the child's age and developmental stage when in an argument. Older children need to feel that they have a voice and that their opinions matter. Younger children need to be allowed to express themselves. Refrain from being too authoritarian in resolving issues.

4.Give more focus on positive behaviors

There is often a tendency to give more attention to negative behaviors that parents overlook the good ones. Children take advantage of this. They act up, throw tantrums, and whine just to get attention. Remember that you are reinforcing the behavior that you most often give attention to. If you want your child to behave a certain way, give more notice to that particular one. Ignore the ones you do not want to happen again.

Praising the child for good behavior results in better conduct than scolding negative ones. The child feels good about the self, and the good conduct is reinforced. The attention gained is also favorable for the child. Children will repeat behaviors that result in making them feel good. Both parties benefit from this setup.

5. Redirect negative behaviors

Children learn to ignore and tune out parents who say "No" and "Don't" all time. Instead, give the child an activity that is more desirable for both. Children are easily distracted, and it is easier to redirect the behavior than to dwell on the misdeed. Disciplining children need not be stressful. You can make it fun by offering enjoyable, challenging activities that teach good behavior. A child running around can be told to try and walk on tiptoes. Then give praise as a positive reinforcement. Make things fun for the child while redirecting the attention away from the negative deeds. When the child scatters toys, instead of telling him not to, engage him in a fun challenge on how fast he can bring the toys back into the box.

Chapter 7

Conventional marriage is on the way out. The whole institution is in trouble. I bring this up because of the dangers this poses to children. There really can be no doubt that the social symptoms of marital misery is everywhere. Symptoms are extremely important to understand when it comes down to family discipline, raising children properly in a loving environment, and most of all, providing them with a positive role model for their own personal reference.

In today's social structure, there happens to be an alarming trend which affects everyone's lives. This is particularly true where child development is concerned. Fatherhood is slowly being destroyed. Now you might not like to hear this but the truth is all around. A social seduction has become well established where the he-man type father is just a figment. A clever method of partisan reason has elevated sophistication into a play-boy attitude and that now seems to be the manly thing.

Results of this cultural adjustment has severe consequences, especially for children. That great leader and authority figure that young developing minds admire seems to have vanished. Replacements are men who no longer feel guilt for cheating on their wives. They have extramarital relationships and mistresses not realizing just how much they destroy home life and making null and void their potential for true fatherhood. They have no time for their wives or children to build a solid foundation and good home. Rather they're in the busy pursuit of chasing the all-mighty dollar and enriching their selfish lives with wine, women, and song (you get what I mean).

Women also have absorbed and parlayed a particular negative attitude as a result. I hear, "no man's going to tell me what to do." Headstrong arrogances drive their husbands away. When they feel intimidated, insulted, and ridiculed, he's not content and when home life is not comfortable he stays away. The children suffer, the home disintegrates, and that's because no one admits to or realizes that motherhood and fatherhood makes for one significant blended loving authority.

Nothing takes the place of a family built around a strong, solid, and close loving marriage. There's plenty of talk about the institution being obsolete. But marriage, legally and socially, is essential to a proper home environment. In essence, marriage supports strong domestic leaders who manage good behavior that essentially showcases strong upper-hand guidance, eliminating the need for physical reprimand.

Ask yourself why the institution of marriage has become unsatisfactory to so many. Do you understand what's behind the preoccupation? Young people are now being conditioned and basically disillusioned with the whole idea of traditional marriage.

Not at all surprising are symptoms that point to one central factor. There's a manifestation of a single problem. I know just how hard this is to admit or realize, but the real answer to this question is dullness and monotony.

This does not, in any way, mean that couples are unhappy. There's some sort of barrier that happens when children are involved. Usually it begins with lack of intimacy, mutual love, understanding, and dedication. That's when wondering eyes begin searching for more exciting things. And children sense dissatisfaction, react to it, and usually end up suffering the consequences.

Ideally, a happy state of matrimony keeps a family alive. It grows with a sparkle and interest. To get there, marital values must not be broken to keep the cheerfulness going. With these noticeable glad tidings come happy and obedient children.

The family is the foundation of any and all societies. Deficiencies need to be dealt with in a logical and loving way, especially for the sake of child discipline and parental respect. If a widow, for instance, is left to raise boys, it would be helpful to point them to good masculine examples in the local community (Boy's club, etc.) They instinctually will copy these men's lives in the most positive way. The same principles apply for girls having positive and loving role models.

Chapter 8: How The Challenge Of Single Parenting Affects Your Decision To Divorce

Single parenting has seemingly become an acceptable norm which is unfortunate. According to the US Census Bureau, there were over 20 million single parents in the United States in the year 2000. That's a staggering statistic, certainly the worldwide number of people who are challenged with single parenting is exponentially higher.

When making a divorce decision and you have children, it is natural to wonder about the challenges of single parenting and how it will affect your children. You may have seen other people struggle with single parenting or thought about the strain single parenting would seemingly put on you and your children.

Single Parenting Is Easier If You Know Yourself

When deciding about getting a divorce and thinking about how single parenting figures in, make sure that you know yourself. Ask yourself if you're really ready to get divorced and if you can overcome the fear or challenge of single parenting. Don't be hasty with your decision, who knows? Maybe your marriage can be saved.

Know whether or not you're thinking of single parenting solely to take something away from your spouse. Clearly a selfish and useless reason to be a single parent. Know whether or not you can adequately be a single parent based on your inner strength, work ethic, tendencies towards being overly busy, etc.

Single parenting is tough, what you may be able to take for granted as a married person will be gone if you're thinking of trying single parenting. Chances are if you're thinking of trying single parenting, you won't have much time at all for yourself. In essence, your 'self' will be all about your children. Know whether you're really ready for this. After all your children deserve the best care possible!

Single Parenting Is Easier If You Know Your Children

Yes, you have to really know your children...you have to know how they'll respond to a plethora of changes if you're going to try single parenting.

How will they respond to not seeing your spouse? Mom or Dad, as often? How will your children react to having to be dropped off at your ex-spouses house for visitation? How will the children feel about potentially not enjoying the same luxuries or attention that they may have had previously? Of course, there's more questions to ask to fit your particular situation. Keep your children's best interest at heart.

You absolutely must know your children in order to be comfortable about trying single parenting. Granted, it won't be easy and there will be rocky points in the process, but if you know your children well enough single parenting can be productive assuming your marriage cannot be saved. In any event, your children most likely will have to sacrifice if you're going to try single parenting.

Single Parenting Will Be Easier If You Review Your Finances And Plan Accordingly

Whether the concept is shallow or not is irrelevant. Finances (or lack thereof) figure in to your decision to venture into single parenting. Take a hard look at what your finances will allow for if you're thinking of becoming a single parent.

You must not let emotion completely rule your decision to try single parenting. In order to do what's best for you and your children, you need to assess just how you'll make ends meet and how you'll provide for them and yourself!

Be sensible and take a good amount of time to figure out how you'll live, where the money will come from, how your own freedoms will be compromised, and more importantly, how your children's freedoms will be affected! If you have a well laid out plan with regards to finance before you start single parenting, you will be much better off.

Single parenting is hard and your children will be affected no matter how well off you are in your life with regards to finance and support mechanisms.

But, unfortunately, single parenting can be a necessary thing to do in some instances. Just do right by your children and yourself and think about the future and how you can build your life correctly before you venture into single parenting.

Chapter 9: Co-Parenting For Two

In a storybook world, children have two loving parents and they all live together in a 2-story with a white picket fence. In the real world, the divorce rate exceeds 50% and that means the parental role is frequently shared over two households.

Divorce often includes anger, resentment, revenge and a host of other negative energies. The emotional upheaval of divorce is enough for a child to absorb without adding ongoing negativity. It's important to picture a divorce from a child's level—and to understand the alienation they feel when their world falls apart.

Frequently children feel that they are somehow responsible for a marriage falling apart. They reason that someone was "bad" and the fact that they love their parents unconditionally, suggests that the parents are not at fault. That leaves the children themselves. If this isn't enough, parents often use their children as tools to leverage the emotional weight that this extreme separation includes. The result is confusion; it is a game that no one wins.

Naturally, neither parent wants this to happen. Their unhappiness and sense of marital failure is tempered with resolve to keep their children safe and loved. Their natural instinct is to be sacrificing—often weighing the logic of splitting up against that of quiet suffering.

The effect of divorce is not just emotional; it frequently involves financial suffering on all the involved parties. Households that formerly rested on two working shoulders, may now rest on one. Separate living means living expenses, cars, meals, holidays; with each parent struggling to be a mirror image of the other.

Bring to this the possibility that each or both parent establishes new relationships and suddenly there may be four parents and eight grandparents; perhaps even new siblings, some unrelated and some newly added to the mix.

Obviously the odds are that this turmoil is going to have a negative effect upon the children involved. It is up to the parents to reduce, or even eliminate the chance. Just as they had the power to separate, they have the power to hold it all together. All it takes is some planning, some selflessness and some control. It can be done with love.

Learn Self-Control

One of the first things to remember is that children do love unconditionally. They do not see faults; they accept them. What is more, they seek approval and reinforcement from their parents, grandparents and even extended family. To find fault with their family members, and most particularly their parent, is to tell the child that their judgment is flawed, rather than the person at whom the anger is directed. They personalize the dissatisfaction they feel about them.

Thus it is very important that adult conversations be conducted behind closed doors and out of hearing. If you need to discuss personal behavior, do it in a business-like manner when the child may be able to witness it, and save the negative emotions for completely private moments. If at all possible, accept your new life and dwell on the positives of the future rather than the perceived faults of the past.

Remember that children are highly perceptive and can pick up on the subtleties, including body language and voice. Long before they were able to speak they relied on gestures, posture and intonation of your voice to communicate. They probably know you better than you know yourself. Pay attention to how you behave when you're angry. Is your breathing rapid? Does your voice elevate in pitch? Do your shoulders tense and do your eyes fixate? Do you reach for a cookie, cigarette, or a pencil? Do you softly tap a toe or a finger?

If you and your ex meet regularly, such as he/she picking up the kids after a visit – consider video taping the meeting. Play it back first with the volume off and focus on the body language. Then play it again and close your eyes – listen to your voice. This is what the children are seeing and hearing. Is it an interaction appropriate for them?

Provide a Secure Environment

When divorce occurs it leaves both parties with the responsibility of taking care of themselves independently. That means that formerly shared duties, like staying with the children while the other is working, are now up to the single parent. That's a huge adjustment for everyone involved. If possible ask someone the child knows very well, particularly family members, to help with the childcare. It's better for children to have fewer interruptions in their day-to-day lives.

If the children will be shuttled between parents, let them choose a few familiar things to take with them, or perhaps even leave in each place. This encourages an atmosphere of sharing and simply spreading the family circle rather than splitting it in half. For example, if you are buying pajamas, buy two pair of the same, or maybe one in each of two colors. This gives the child a sense of continuity between both locations.

At this point, let's talk a bit about competition between parents. Your child is not a bargaining chip. They did not ask for a divided family. There is nothing positive to be gained from putting them between battling adults. Respect their right to a peaceful environment. It's not a good idea to use them to deliver verbal messages.

If you and your ex cannot be amicable, consider in seeing a licensed counselor who can bring some moderation to the situation. Working out a mutually agreeable set of rules can bring peace when you need it most.

Remember...judges and child court respect good parenting skills.

If yours is an only child, consider getting them a cuddly puppy. Caring for a pet gives them a sense of control and allows them to develop their own care giving tendencies. A warm puppy can be a confidante and a protector when it grows. Be sure the breed selection is shared between each parent so the new addition is welcomed in either household.

Learn How to Communicate

Negotiating a family divorce calls for your best diplomatic skills.It can be very confusing when you are trying to sort out behavior adjustments from being totally open and intimate with a partner one moment and to consider them the opposition the next. It is a good idea to conduct a meeting that has only to do with the children—leave other issues behind. In this meeting, establish some ground rules for behavior and communications. Agree to be positive and pro-active when it comes to anything regarding the children. Determine how you will handle situations like parent-teacher conferences, school events, church, holidays, in-laws and grandparents in-laws, new family relationships, birthdays, clothing, vacations and so forth. Knowing in advance how to plan prevents conflicts and bickering. This is not only true for the parents and children, but the extended family, school, neighbors and more.

Discuss child support and how you expect to handle it, and even how to handle the lack of it. Sudden unemployment or illness can affect support payments – on both sides. It's not deliberate, but just one of those golden opportunities life offers to build character. The children love both parents, no matter who is paying the bills. Their welfare and happiness must come first.

Learn how to communicate with your children. Meet with them jointly to maintain the family unit as far as they are concerned. Encourage open discussion and avoid plotting or revenge, on everyone's part. Establish some sort of forum in which difficulties can be expressed and worked out. Perhaps this will be in the form of a quiet, public place such as a café; somewhere that good behavior is expected. Perhaps it is a weekly conference telephone call. If verbal discussion is out of the question, consider involving an outside impartial person—this could be a respected extended family member, a good family friend, a cleric or a counselor. When all else fails, set up a blackboard in an accessible location like the garage where either party can leave notes, requests, instructions and maintain a calendar. There are even Internet options such as Google where each party can contribute to a central message board and calendar, pictures and more.

On a sober, but very important note, good communication also involves good planning. Be sure to update wills, life insurance beneficiaries, college fund contributions and other policies, programs and life planning activities that affect the children.

Chapter 10: Planning To Go Solo

There are times when people who are financially accomplished decide to add to their wish list. You have worked very hard to earn all you have and then you realise that all along, your biological clock was not running slower than that of your contemporaries. You have cushioned and handsomely rewarded yourself with all that your heart ever desired except for one thing, having a child of your own!

Only if having a child were as easy as purchasing a piece of property, then one would be spared all the headaches and related stress that goes with it! Now you are faced with a million and one questions, which are not easy to answer. Who is the most suitable and worthy partner with whom to have a child? Men tend to be more cruel and selfish than women when it comes to answering this question. All they do is pick a particular woman, comply with all the love routine (check all the boxes), go through all the HIV and other related tests so that they can entice their prey. Before a woman can suspect any foul play, he has found a perfect way of dumping you and file for sole custody of the child, which was his plan from the onset anyway. The woman on the other hand continues to ask herself questions like, must I get a man to father a child for me or must I get myself a sperm donor? When the child is born, should I use my surname or the father's to identify the child? Will I cope with the sleepless nights and morning sickness all by myself without the support of the child's father during pregnancy? Is it possible for a woman to be frank with a man she likes to ask him to simply give her a child and have him stay out of the child's life forever? Is there a man that is emotionally and intellectually mature enough to handle such a frank "selfish" request? If I do get a sperm donor, would I be satisfied having limited information about the father of my child and have no family contacts at all to help me better understand some of the hereditary mannerisms and peculiar demeanour this child will possess from his/her father's ancestry?

In the event that you choose not to involve the man in the life of your child during your pregnancy, how are you planning to manoeuvre your way around the temptation to involve him later on, especially when you might be forced to involve him against your will? Okay then, suppose you have all these questions adequately covered including the moral and ethical ones that you uphold for both your spiritual and intellectual sanity, what is now stopping you from executing your plan? I firmly believe that a person that is sold to his/her own convictions in the context of his/her immediate society stands a better chance of making success of many decisions compared to a double minded one. All we need to remember when we decide to have children is that children are offshoots of a broader community and as such, they must not be treated like pets. You are planning to raise a human-B.E.I.N.G not a soulless animal! Dare I say it again; your plan is to raise a human-INDIVIDUAL unique in every respect. So do yourself a favour and purposely ponder upon your decision with great care. It may just happen that you soon find yourself in a difficult position where you need to answer questions of identity and the like from the child you are now planning to have. It is better to have peace of mind about such an important undertaking than to simply dive in and then live with regrets thereafter. Take into account all factors within your social context; things like religious beliefs, morality, norms and ethics because soon you will be expected to pass the same to this newcomer you are planning to have and raise.

Chapter 11: Rules Of Thumb-Length Of

Time

As a very general rule, a child's Time Out should be one minute for every year of the child's developmental age. It is very important to consider the child in terms of their various developmental parts when determining the length of time for a Time Out. A five year old may not be five in all areas of their development. You must adjust the time to their needs. We had a foster child in our home once who was 12 chronologically, but 6 emotionally. This impacted the type and length of interventions we could use. I often found myself trapped between looking at the 12 year old and talking to the 6 year old. Reminding myself to respond to her youngest level of development kept me

from irrationally reacting to her and allowed me to remain a joyful parent. If I had followed the "One minute per Year" rule, I would have given a six year old a twelve minute Time Out, which would have been punishing to both of us rather than a nurturing and teaching opportunity. Therefore, it is critical to assess your child's development. It is equally important to assess the speed of their de-escalation. Your child may calm faster than you expect, or she may take longer than you ever dreamed.If you are not tuned-in to BOTH—development AS WELL AS the rate of de-escalation—you will miss the critical opportunity to nurture and teach.
-Location

The location of the Time Out can be anywhere that the child and adult can be separated from distractions and focus on what is happening with the child. Therefore, Time Out does not need to be held in a closet, laundry room, or any other out-of-the-way location. It just needs to be private, and the more neutral the territory, the better. The LAST place that Time Out should happen is in the child's room. This space is too familiar, comforting, and personal to the child. Do not send the child to their room thinking it is a time out.It will only result in a sense of abandonment or a sense of escape or vacation, especially if the child's room has been loaded with electronics, books, games, etc.

Ideally, you would conduct the Time Out in the location that the event was occurring.It is not worth the battle of relocation when the child is upset.One very effective way to achieve privacy and to remove distraction is to have all other people leave the room. This will help the child and you engage in the calming and reengagement process of the Time Out so that you can achieve the maximum growth from the teaching opportunity.Do not let yourself get tied to the notion that the Time Out must be on "THE" bench or chair.

The only caveat to this is if the need for Time Out occurs in a public place, such as at the store. The social shame and ridicule that could result will be far more punishing than the attempted discipline. In such situations, you must first ask, "Why do I care?" If you are giving the Time Out or getting upset because of the social implications of the other adults looking at you, you are engaging for the wrong reasons. The other thing that must be considered in a store or public location is the boredom or over stimulation the child may be experiencing. Perhaps the whole reason they are having trouble is the environment itself.

-Instructions

The child needs to be able to focus on the action that created the Time Out and to reflect on the possible future choices they can make. I have been amazed by the insight even children as young as two or three years old can express during the reflection process. When their brains are calm, children can be very insightful, and can be very effectively guided by the adult.

Keep the rules basic:

1. Stay in your chair, on the bench, pillow, etc.

2. Think about why a Time Out is needed.

3. Calm down.

4. Think of ways that you can avoid a Time Out next time.

The main intent of the Time Out is to help the child calm down and to give them (and YOU!) a chance to consider alternative actions. Do not get caught in the trap of seeing the Time Out as the event itself. Sitting and separating the child from the event is only the beginning—nothing more than the "reset button" of emotional arousal. Be aware that if your child has escalated to the point that you feel he needs a Time Out, he will likely be physically agitated, adrenaline-charged, and have a very difficult time calming down. In reality, being upset that your child cannot calm and is physically active is like being upset that you got wet when you went swimming! Trying to parent while you or your child are in the midst of such illogical emotions creates the potential for punishment and significantly narrows the opportunity for nurture. So it is imperative that you consider your own reaction to stress and agitation. Is your heart pounding and your need to pace or move risen? Now, observe your child. Look for clues about the child's physical state and needs. If the child is full of adrenaline, let him burn it off by walking with you, throwing something, or even jumping on a trampoline.Even positive activities like these can serve as a Time Out, allowing you to engage the child and soothe her physiological needs, resulting in good parent-child time. Some have renamed this positive spin on Time Out, calling it "Time In."Utilizing this approach invites you to find joy with the child as the child reclaims their emotional control.

Remember that the primary purpose of Time Out is to allow the child to de-escalate and re-engage the logical cortex of his brain. On the way down he will pass through the emotional brain and slowly re-enter cognitive (thinking) functioning. When you see that the child has entered what I term "emotional refraction," you have met the goal of the Time Out and are now ready to teach. What do I do while the child is calming? While the child is in a Time Out, it is a great time for you to calm yourself if the event caused you to get upset. You can also contemplate what a logical and natural consequence for the behavior is. Finally, you need to remain connected to the child in order observe their calming so you can seize the teaching moment. It is vital that you attend fully to your child during the Time Out is vital so that you can appropriately intervene when the moment strikes. The most important thing for you during the Time Out is to remain within the child's field of vision. Your presence helps the child calm down and stay on task.

Rules For the Adult

1. Stay calm and remain the "adult". We do not need two children in the room. Ask yourself the three questions, and allow yourself time to fully answer them.

2. Remain present with the child, but do not engage the child except to redirect and to calm. Reacting validates and encourages the inappropriate attention-seeking behaviors.

3. Redirect the child gently. Remind him that the time will start when he is quietly sitting. (It is possible to have a very long Time Out if the child will not calm down. Remember to meet the physical needs as well.)

4. End the Time Out as soon as you see the child enter a state of emotional refraction. This does not always take the full time and is not the same as just being quiet. By being present with the child you will sense the shift and know they have entered a teaching state.

5. Remind yourself that you are nurturing and redirecting, not punishing. This helps when the child is belligerent and verbally ugly.

6. As soon as the child enters emotional refraction, the teaching can begin, and you have the opportunity to nurture, reassure, and instruct a child who is now able to listen, learn, and respond.

Chapter 12: When & Why Our Words

Matter

As a child, we too looked up to our parents; we hanged on to every word they said and every action they do. And we have to admit: most of the time they were right – we just had to learn it the hard way. Now that we've become parents ourselves, a pressing question for us is: how should we relate in such a way that brings our children closer to us?

For that, we can get answers from our childhood. Let's reflect on when we chose to listen to our parents, and when not. What were they doing 'wrongly'?

Every family has their own communication style. However, there are some common factors behind effective parental-child communication.

In the preceding chapter, we discussed how we can adjust our way of thinking so that it fits with our child's view of the world, for the sake of understanding their behavior and shaping our response to effect positive changes. Communication, after all, becomes a better experience when everyone is on the same page.

Toxic Phrases We Should Avoid Using With Our Kids

Let's start off with common phrases we should all avoid using:

"I'm going to leave you if…" – This is one of the most dangerous phrases we could ever say to our child. This teaches them the notion that love is conditional, when it really shouldn't be. Often times it can be effective in the short-term in modifying behavior as we're unwittingly toying with the child's fear of being left alone, and of taking safety away from them. However, this is a dangerous strategy as it can have serious negative repercussions on the child's development. They'll do what you say out of fear instead of understanding the logic behind whatever you're telling them. This is a great disservice to their learning of the ways of the world. Instead of bringing our child closer to us, this creates a false belief in the child that he or she would only be loved so long as they do what they're told.

"That's bad..." – Even as adults we don't really like hearing this particular phrase, as it has such a rich negative connotation. Saying "That person is bad so don't talk to him" or "Stop doing that, it's bad!" may give children the impression that the world is simply a black or white place, without shades of grey. If it's not good then it's bad, if you're not good then you're bad. Using this phrase may have adverse effects on how your child views the world, and may reduce your child's ability to take into account the complexities of the world when shaping his or her opinions and decisions.

"Do's and Don'ts" – It's important that we teach our kids things that should and should not be done, especially when it concerns their safety and well-being. Educating your child on why it is not healthy to bite his nails is essential, for one. However, sometimes we tend to over-use these two words and ended up being perceived by the child as being dictatorial. The child simply does not understand why certain behaviors are allowed, while others are not. It's not that we cannot tell our children what is in their best interests, but the choice of words we use, and the way we say it, has a big impact on how it ends up being perceived by them.

Instead of saying 'don't bite your nails, it's not good for you' or 'it's dirty to bite your nails', educate your child by teaching them what's bacteria and how biting their nails can lead to stomachache. We will relate to them better by framing our intentions in a way that they can easily comprehend. For instance, for the above example, we can begin by portraying bacteria as monsters, and how they would not want to have monsters in their stomach!

However, when we fail to relate to our kids, and overuse words such as 'do not', we are presenting our child a dichotomy of what they can and cannot do. Telling our sons "boys don't cry" or our daughters "it is only natural that girls help do the laundry" reinforces common stereotypes that are unhelpful. Let's give them enough freedom to choose and the space to make informed decisions as long as it will not cause harm unto themselves or to others.

"I'll hate you if you.../I'll love you if you..." – Again, this is an open declaration of conditional love that imprints on our child the idea that it is necessary to do or not to do certain things in order to gain someone's affection. Saying things such as "I'll hate you if you keep crying" will put too much pressure on our little ones. This may breed insecurity in them when, say, they fail to meet a certain expectation. That insecurity saps at their self-confidence and hinders them from exploring new horizons in fear of losing your affection. This negative dynamic will also inevitably rear its ugly head in their relationships with others.

"I'll give you a (insert reward here) if you..." – Although the reward system is a pretty effective way to modify behavior as researched by renowned American psychologist B.F. Skinner (2), it can seriously backfire if done incorrectly. Rewards usually need to be given intermittently without following a specific pattern; children may only be rewarded with due cause. If rewards are given so frequently, after every task finished, it may result in two undesirable outcomes: (One) Your child only obeys you if some sort of reward is involved or (Two) the reward loses its effect and appeal in motivating your child's behavior.

Use These Positive Phrases Instead

What then are some of the words we can use to encourage positive behavior and improve our emotional bond with our children?

Positive parenting words fall under three broad categories:

Words of Encouragement – As hard as it may be, I believe it is vital to focus on and encourage continued good behavior in our children. When we focus on pointing out our children's good behavior and frequently express our appreciation for it, they will feel encouraged to continue the same positive behavior. This leads to positive reinforcement, whereby one positive action is followed by a reinforcing stimulus (such as verbal praise, a new toy, or any other reward), making it more likely that the behavior will occur again in the future. We can dish out sincere compliments such as 'That's my good girl!", "Well done! You've done me proud!" or "Mummy really likes it when you keep your toys after playing with them!" in response to good behavior. That conveys your expectations in a loving way instead of simply saying "you should always keep your toys after playing with them!".

Words of Empowerment – Ask around and almost every parent would tell you that it is easier to build good habits in children when they're much younger. According to a recent study in the United States by Brown University (3), routines and habits – including household chores and responsibility – take root in children by age 9.That means we have a precious window of opportunity to help our kids cultivate healthy habits. And one of the most important habits we can help cultivate in them is to consciously build a positive and empowering mindset. We start off by using words of empowerment more often, in ways that boosts confidence in our kids' own ability to get things done and effect positive changes in their lives. It is crucial to use words of empowerment to encourage continued progress and self-confidence during critical developmental stages in our children's lives.

For instance, when we see our toddlers taking the first steps in their lives, or getting the first 'A' grade in class, or even remembering who Aunt Lucy or Uncle Johnny is. An example of words of empowerment includes: "You have improved and are doing even better than the last time you've tried this!". Using empowering words more often would cause young children to associate you with feeling good about themselves, thus bringing you closer together.

Words of Trust – Some parents may find it difficult to trust their kids to take good care of themselves or to do the right thing, especially when they're still at a young age. However, it is precisely because of their young age that it's crucial we begin using words of trust to cultivate a sense of self-responsibility – and ultimately, independence – in them. Words of trust convey the belief and confidence that we have in our kids to know how and when to do the right thing for themselves. An example would be 'I'm sure you know how to pack your bags like we did the last time!". This instills in kids the value of taking responsibility for one's life.

How Fighting Fire With Fire Leads To An Inferno

One thing I'm confident we can all agree upon is that children do tend to push your limits! I understand that sometimes you feel like giving into the temptation and just throw a fit yourself or tear a wall down. But please, don't!

We've all been there and we all know that will not end well.

The key to getting the upper hand in these kinds of situation is to get on your children's shoes and contemplate: If I were a 5-years-old, how can I make myself listen?

The answer? Don't fight fire with fire. We fight it with three of the other basic elements – earth, water, and air.

Earth – Specifically, remain down-to-earth (i.e. remain centered). The one who gets angered and agitated loses the game. Leverage on what you know about your child – his likes, dislikes, or interests – to effect changes in his behavior. Let him pick up his toys before watching his favorite TV show or allow him to make his bed for a fresh box of Cheerios with a free toy inside! The idea is to remain centered despite the fact that you may be boiling on the inside. That allows you to see the situation for what it is, and to get a better grip of it.

Water – Instead of getting hot-headed, be as cool as a can of cola! As mentioned previously, kids love getting your attention – in every possible way. They'd get the steam run up your head just to have you take notice of them. So instead of reacting in a knee-jerk way, be wary of over-reacting.

Air – Give them air – or space, to be exact. When a child is in the middle of an episode, it is best to first physically remove them from the trigger. This gives them the space to then calm down. If he or she is throwing a fit inside a shopping mall, when appropriate, go to the parking lot and give them all the space they need to collect their thoughts. We don't have to try and make them stop either. Simply bring them away from the place that is causing them discomfort, give them space to talk, and listen intently. When we do that, we may learn more about what is it that is bothering them than when we reprimand them inside the mall! Sometimes, giving them a breather goes a long way!

Building Our Own Communication Blueprint

As we try different methods in managing our children's behavior, we will eventually identify a pattern of triggers, behaviors, and how our own words and reactions have an impact upon that behavior. These patterns are useful in helping us build our communication blueprint.

But what exactly is a communication blueprint, and how does it help in our endeavor to raise happy and disciplined kids who are emotionally-close to us?

A communication blueprint is a plan of communication that is specifically-designed to suit our unique circumstances. It is designed based on a deep understanding of one's communication style and patterns, and how that impacts our relationships with others. Having one's own communication blueprint helps identify potential areas of conflict and misunderstanding, and serves as a guide for us to navigate smoothly around them. If designed and used correctly, it helps to cultivate a closer relationship where everyone involved feels heard and understood, and their concerns taken into account.

Kids want to feel heard and understood, and they want to feel safe. Having any of that taken away would usually lead to child tantrums. By building and following our own communication blueprint, we make our kids feel heard, understood, and safe.

The following lists great and enlightening questions that we can ask of ourselves when building a communication blueprint. The list is not exhaustive:

- What makes our child happy? What are some of the happiest moments we've seen our kids had, and is there a common factor behind it? For instance, in my family, I've observed that my kids are the most joyous when both my husband and I bring them out for an outdoor activity. It can be as simple as a picnic, or teaching them how to cycle in the park. I believe that identifying this is crucial in helping us plan more of such activities that bring our kids joy, and bring us closer together.

- What makes our child 'tick'? Of all the tantrum episodes, what are the common triggers? Is it the child's perceived lack of concern from me? Is it when the child is asked to engage in a new activity without my active participation?

- How does my child respond when he / she is happy or upset? And for the latter, how do we usually deal with it? Have I remained centered and calm, or have I been reacting in a knee-jerk way? How has that been working for me thus far?

- How have I been responding to my child throwing a tantrum? What choice of words have I used? Has it been effective? Have I been loving towards my child or have I unwittingly used coercion ("If you don't keep your toys after playing with them, you won't get to play them again!") to try to effect change in their behavior?

- How has my child reacted to my choice of words under those circumstances? Do I feel that my words have encouraged positive changes in their behavior or has the situation only gotten worse? Do I feel that my kids have 'pulled away' (emotionally disengaged) from me since?

- What positive words can I use to compliment my child for good behavior?

- What encouraging words can I use on my child to change his / her behavior for the better?

Chapter 13: Unleashing Your Child's

Imaginative And Creative Power

35 years of extensive scientific research have validated the notion that an emphasis on a person's intellect and intelligence does not help that person become successful in life.

When you constantly stress how unintelligent a child is, it reinforces the mindset that intellect is innate and cannot be acquired or improved upon. Thus, instead of your child working on polishing his or her intelligence, and improving his or her skills, the child starts taking it for granted and fails to put in the effort needed to amplify it.

Such was the case of Jonathan, a brilliant student until he reached grade seven and failed to perform better after that. Deep research on his case discovered his parents never worked on developing a growth mindset in him and never encouraged him to unlock his creative power. Since he did not know that creativity was an element that needed discovery, and intelligence was an acquired trait, he simply stopped striving to be better.

If you do not want to make the same mistake Jonathan's parents did, it is essential you work towards unleashing your child's imaginative and creative power. So how do you unleash your child's imaginative and creative power?

How To Unleash Your Child's Imaginative And Creative Power

Here's how to unleash and develop your child's imaginative and creative power.

Arrange creative activities

One useful and highly effective technique you can use to unlock your child's ability to be innovative and imaginative is to arrange exciting, creative activities. Start doing this when your child turns three so that you can train him or her to be innovative from a tender age. The earlier you develop this ability, the easier it will be for your child to think innovatively. Some creative activities ideas include:

Painting Activities: Give your child a few colors of paint and many interesting objects, such as blocks, leaves, feathers, toothbrush, sponges, and a normal paintbrush. Give your child lots of papers to create art on, and join your child in creating the art; take any object and start painting with it and let your child follow your example.

Do not guide, or tell your child which object to pick, or what to draw. Let the child do what he or she wants and keep the praise coming in so that he or she can be motivated to come up with fresh ideas. You will be surprised at what amazing creations your toddler can create.

Make creations using cardboard boxes: This activity is great for children aged five and above. Give your child cardboard boxes of different sizes, tape, lots of markers, stickers, and ribbons. Ask your child to do whatever he or she wants with those boxes. As stated above, do not guide your child; simply let your child follow his or her imagination. He or she might end up making a castle, or a car, or something truly unique, of his or her own creation. This activity teaches your children to be creative and independent at the same time.

Be imaginative with play dough: Give your child play dough to make different creations. Let your child enjoy the different textures of the materials. Make sure to keep your child engrossed in this activity by appreciating his or her work.

Read your child stories: Reading fantasy and other sorts of fiction stories to your child is a great way to stimulate his or her creative power. When you read stories to your child, the child begins imagining the characters described in the stories, which in turn helps unlock the child's creative ability.

After reading a story, ask your child to draw how they think the castle would look like, or how the fiery dragon would look like. Your child is definitely going to come up with something different from what you thought. This will indicate that your child's creative ability and imagination is vibrantly healthy and constantly developing.

Play the imagination game: When you sit down for some quality time with your child, play the imagination game. Give your child any scene from a story or movie he or she likes and ask the child to think how he or she would act in that situation.

This gives your child a chance to think out of the box and express his or her ideas. It is important to be very encouraging and if your child births a volatile or violent idea, carefully guide him or her without being too loud or harsh with the child.

Play with blocks: Buy many blocks for your child to play with them as these tools unlock your child's innovative power. A recently conducted study by researchers at the University of Washington located in Seattle studied the effect of playing with blocks on toddlers.

The researchers gave a group of toddlers wooden blocks to play with; after six months, the researchers asked that group and another control group of toddlers who did not use any blocks to take language development tests. The results showed that the group that played with blocks had a 15 percent better result than that of the control group.

Let your child lead the play: If you consistently direct your child on what to do, or not do during his or her playtime, stop doing that. Let your child lead his or her playtime. This helps the child create make-believe games, which is a great tactic to develop and enhance your child's creativity.

Do new things every week: It is important to have family rituals, so your child bonds with you and learns the importance of developing norms and rituals in the family; but it is also substantially important to spice up your child's life. Engage your child in something new each week so things do not become monotonous.

Expert psychologists state that a monotonous routine can often hamper a child's imaginative power. Therefore, ensure to spice up your child's routines. Take your child to a new park, create a new game, or try a new food every week.

Reinvent routine objects: Make sock bunnies, cardboard castles, and play telephones out of cans. This helps your child reinvent routine objects and become amazingly creative. Once you child's creative power is unleashed, your child can thrive in the most difficult life situations.

Arrange play dates: It is important to let your child mingle with other children his or her age. Doing this helps your child develop his or her social skills and enhances his or her creativity. Play dates are a great way for your child to learn new ideas from other children, and interpret these ideas into creative, imaginative ideas of your child's making.

Implement these ideas into your child's routine to help your child become amazingly innovative. When your child's creative abilities expand, his or her growth mindset enhances.

After your child becomes creative and innovative, he or she will be bursting with ideas. At this point, your child will show interest in specific things; perhaps your child will show a keen interest in certain games or activities such as painting, story time, etc.

When this happens, you need to be recognize what interests your child because this could be your child's passion: it is every parent's duty to develop a child's natural ability. In the next section, we shall examine how to help your child realize his or her talents and passions.

Chapter 14: Toddler Proofing

Preventing an awful incident from happening is always a lot better than trying to resolve it. Finding a resolution to a conflict is always tougher, more laborious, and more emotionally taxing. That is why toddler proofing a home is a better alternative and you should take measures to do it.

More Yes's Please!

As stated earlier, a lot of these tantrums occur simply because your child did not get what he or she wants. That means that you should arrange things so that you don't have to say no all the time. That is a lot easier to do at home than outside the home. That is basically the idea behind child proofing or toddler proofing your home.

So, how do you toddler proof your house? The first step is to clean up your home.

Find all the stuff that your toddler can break. Your home should have been baby proofed when your child was born, remember?

Anything that can harm your child should be out of reach. That includes vases that can be knocked down, anything that can break, anything that you don't want your kids to put into their mouths, and anything that is valuable that can get ruined or destroyed if it becomes a toy.

If we try to make a list of things it may be quite long. Well, here's a partial list: pots, vases, picture frames, game consoles, tools, knives, trophies, ceramics, fish bowls, your Playstation, Xbox, cell phones, skateboards, jewelry, chalk, sketch pads, collector's item car miniatures, sports equipment, gardening tools, make up, lipstick, chess pieces, and a lot of other stuff.

Locking Up and Blocking Up

Of course you don't want your toddler to just go anywhere inside the house. Some parts of the home may look innocent but they may pose a threat to a youngster. For instance, if you have a pool in the backyard, you should make sure that your young child will never have direct access to it. If you need to fence it off temporarily then do it.

Some places like the garage and the basement should always be closed and if possible kept under lock and key. Your kitchen smells nice and it's often clean but it is also where you keep your cooking utensils (which include your knife and a lot of other sharp and pointy things). You basically need to limit your toddler's access to certain places in the home.

A great tool that you can invest on is safety gates. You can fence off areas of the home so your toddler won't be able to enter there. Your child may try their luck with some of the doors and entry ways but if it remains shut they will usually give up and try something else.

Advantages of Toddler Proofing a Home

Toddler proofing has a few inherent advantages. First off, it reduces the amount of conflict. If your child has a request then you will most likely have to say yes. Since all of the things that he can see and play with are safe for him/her then you just say yes when your child makes a request.

If they want to go somewhere, most of the time they will point to something that isn't fenced off or closed. Again, you will end up saying yes because the safe areas have already been predetermined. There will be fewer stressful situations, which is good for both the parents and their children.

Not Everything Can be Toddler Proofed

Unfortunately you can't toddler proof the whole world. The most you can do is to make your home a safe place for them. When you finally bring them outside there will be instances that you will have to use tantrum management techniques just to control the situation. However, it does pay to know the most common stressors that may trigger a tantrum, which will be discussed in the next chapter.

Chapter 15: Causes Of Parenting Pitfalls

Parents' Innate behaviours

It is not uncommon to find parents under a lot of pressure right from the moment they become parents. **There is this constant belief that children are parents' measure of success and failure.** Children are expected to be perfect so that parents can look successful and parents are continuously seen trying to prevent failures. **This belief, that as parents they are constantly being judged by the people around them,** and that a small mistake will put them into a "bad parent" category, makes them stressful and anxious. The direct effect of such behaviour is on the growth and development of the child.

Individual Weaknesses

More often than not, we see parents who fail to raise mentally and emotionally healthy adults because of their own drawbacks. **The inability to accept change, or accept feedback and criticism leads to defensiveness in parents.** This behaviour leads them into believing that they are always right and the child's opinion or feelings don't matter at all.

For some parents, parenting is all about providing for the child. Significant aspects of parenting, like spending quality time, paying attention to the child and listening to what the child has to say are avoided. **This is usually a result of under confident parents**, who prefer to take the least resistant way. They completely overlook their capability and role in shaping their child's future. No effort is put in understanding what parenting is all about and its eventual goal is ignored.

Flawed Understanding Of The Concept Of Parenting

Parents often set themselves up for disappointment when **they set unrealistic expectations from their chid.** They forget that their child is not born with an impeccable nature and perfect behaviour. These parents are irritable and often berate their child in front of others, and in private all the same. Their **flawed understanding of a child's mind and its growth curve**, cost the child, a whole lot. The child grows up with anxiety and is uneasy in social situations.

Another major cause of bad parenting is **not feeling the need to constantly improve one's parenting skills**. For some parents it is very difficult to accept that good parenting starts from them. **For them somehow, the very fact that they are parents biologically, certifies their readiness and perfection as parents.** They become defensive and fail to accept when they are at fault or when they are expected to step up in the process.

Missteps In Parenting

It has been observed that parents who like to be in control of everything, commonly end up **micro- managing and over controlling their children**. This causes depression and anxiety in children. For example; **authoritarian parents dictate terms and are demanding.** The problem with them is that their demands are never backed by a rationale, and the fact that **they don't encourage communication,** makes the development of a child's understanding of things even worse. The child does not have the freedom to ask questions, therefore she grows up not understanding the concept of rationality. This leads to flawed judgement and incapability to differentiate right from wrong.

When **parents fail to praise their child or fail to give her the parental warmth** that is important for a healthy bond between them, they are setting the child up for social withdrawal and insecurity. A child who doesn't receive love and respect at home often ends up believing that she lacks the ability to be loved and accepted. Such children grow into adults who lack confidence and constantly seek approval from others.

Having talked about the various parenting pitfalls, their causes and their subsequent effect on the growth of the child, it is of utmost importance to understand and ponder over the following:

- Parenting is an ongoing process and there is always scope for growth and improvement.

- Parents will always have baggage from their upbringing and experiences.

- It's up to the parent to decide what it is, that they would want to give their child;

1. A healthy and holistic growth

2. Or a clueless life with no emotional stability and no rationale for judgement.

Open-mindedness and tolerance should be highlighted while parenting. The grown-up should be capable of questioning everything that is taught to her and asked of her. This will make sure that she is able to make relevant choices about religion, education, career, lifestyle etc. not based on what is expected of her, but instead, on her own understanding of these things. Parents should aim their parenting skills towards developing a child who is able to make decisions keeping in mind her growth and development.

Chapter 16: People Considering Having Children

Take parenting classes and read parenting books. The traditional ethos that parenting should come naturally to everyone has been challenged in recent years. Education is helpful for anyone wanting to succeed at any endeavor, and parenting should be no exception. Many people take home economics in junior high and high school, learning how to do everything from make sound financial decisions to cooking and cleaning and maintaining a healthy household. A number of high school students are also taught some sex education, where they may learn about the risks of pregnancy and very little about childcare itself. The notion that schools should teach general life skills, as part of the rest of their curriculum, has been well established. Parenting classes are rarely required learning in high schools, however, and many people approach parenting with minimal experience in caring for children. Becoming self-educated about parenting is easier than ever before.

Anyone interested in learning about proper parenting has a plethora of books available to them, written by everyone from child psychologists to experienced parents, or both. Prospective parents may feel overwhelmed seeing the huge amount of information available today. The Internet has only increased the amount of available perspectives on parenting. Many mothers and fathers have set up blogs about their children and parenting in general, while academics and childcare workers are able to make almost all of their various opinions available to the world. Prospective parents should try to read as much as they can about parenting. Ideally, they should read about child growth and development and different parenting styles, while also reading about the real world experiences of real parents. Theoretical information about childrearing would give anyone a firm basis in understanding children and raising children. Seeing direct examples of childrearing in the real world will give people a different set of valuable evidence.

Prospective parents will feel more confident that they know what they are getting themselves into, and will feel more prepared for the task at hand. Anyone who reads enough books and blogs and takes in enough information will eventually start to notice patterns. Some experiences certain parents have may seem overly specific to them, whereas others will seem like universal parenting experiences when they show up over and over again. Child psychologists may also make similar recommendations often enough that they seem less debatable. Eventually, the truth and theory behind parenting will emerge, and new parents can feel more secure in their resources.

Chapter 17: How To Stop A Biting Child

It is certainly a big challenge and not fun at all when your child is biting others. I know, I was there with one of my own children and it was very frustrating not knowing what to do and how to get her to stop biting.

Something for sure here is that at first I didn't take it as a big deal as I thought it must have been an episode of simple anger but would later stop naturally, and as I did nothing about it I found out she had done it again, and again. So the point here is because I did nothing; it just continued on getting worse.

And so I decided to take action and do something about it. You will find out that the following tips will usually work pretty good and will help out your child to stop biting. But before I get to them, I want to re-emphasize that giving your child love is one of the best things you can do because with that you are showing them you care and you are there and understand what they are going through.

Now that I made that a little more clear, here are some of the best things I learned that will help you help your child to stop biting other little kids:

Teach them that there is a consequence for bad actions. Biting is certainly a bad action to take towards others. Let them know with words that it hurts when others are bitten. If your child is older, you can do something like taking one of their favorite stuffed animals away for a short period of time.

Give your child timeout. I used to put my child facing the wall for about three minutes, as I did this every time she bit someone, or did something else she knew was wrong she began to tell me it was boring to be sitting and staring at the wall and didn't like it. With time, it actually came to be an effective way to program in their little minds, that biting has its consequences.

Use a firm voice to tell them No! Using expressions such as "No biting" is another way to communicate to them that biting is not okay. Make sure you include the action, why "No", in this case, "biting". Also, the use of a firm clear voice, will allow their little minds to absorb the difference in tone of your voice, and associate that with discipline in the long run, so it is important not to use a calm, or normal kind of tone when speaking to them.

Pay more attention to the other child. In a way, this will show them that a consequence of them biting will mean you paying more attention to the child that has been hurt. Although, this is not one of my favorite, it is important to include as different toddlers have different reactions, and this may prove to be an effective one for you to help your child stop biting.

Never reflect the pain back. Some people may recommend giving them a taste of their actions, as a way to teach them what it really does to others; in this case, biting them back! Now, I'm more of a fan in utilizing positive methods rather than negative methods like these because when your toddler is in such a young age when they absorb many of the things they learn during the first years of their life, they tend to carry it for the rest of their life and it becomes harder to deal with negative behaviors later. Not that they will keep on biting other people when they turn ten, but having taught them through the use of negative approaches.

When it comes to biting, the previous tips were the ones I had the most success with. I would strongly recommend resisting negative approaches as much as possible, although sometimes especially after following numerous consistent attempts; you find out you are not having as much success with them. Only then would I recommend proceeding with other negative methods.

How To Deal With Tantrums

You should know that tantrums beginning in the terrible twos phases usually between 18 months to four years of age are a normal part of your toddler's development. Their mind has entered a new world where they start to realize that they can start making their own little decisions, they are exploring their world, and are impatient, hyperactive, curious and excited to find out about their surroundings. As they interact with all these things and with other children they will find it difficult to express exactly what they are feeling, and so this "terrible twos" phase is a common and normal part of their emotional development.

You, as the parent are responsible for influencing and helping your child ease these tantrum episodes because your little one is just not equipped with the maturity and emotional understanding that you as an adult have. It is then important to be active when it comes to your child harming others in the process, and so it is best to be equipped with the necessary understanding on how you can do this.

Begin by making playtime and their environment a safe and fun one to be in. Pay attention to how they act, interact, and react with other children and take action to correct any unacceptable behavior. Unacceptable behaviors that go uncorrected will only continue to get worse and harder to deal with, that is why it is very important for you as the parent to take the right actions to correct it when they happen. Even at this early age, toddlers are already smarter than you think, and they are continuously learning and can see, hear, and feel how you act yourself. Because of this, you must remain calm when approaching your toddler every time a correction needs to be made, you must talk in a normal voice when you are letting them know you understand their frustration, but you must talk in a firm voice when you are communicating discipline to a negative behavior. All these approaches will reflect in how your toddler sees you, hears you and feels about the way you are taking action.

I remember my husband, as many other husbands I am guessing; was a bit more impatient, and tended to utilize a firm voice for just about everything. When there were occasions when we would go out and our child had a tantrum episode, he often proceeded to using his firm voice and took him outside and sometimes inside the car for a more private man to son lesson. But as we found out from experience, it became way more effective when I stepped in and in a very calm manner I talked to our young son. By simply showing I understood his frustration and talking and behaving in a very understanding and calm way, he would calm down and began to use more words to try to describe his frustrations. Being this young it was difficult for him to communicate how he felt or what he wanted and even more difficult to understand why a dad may have been using his firm voice on him when all he wanted was to sit next to mom, yet here is daddy with his big firm voice correcting him because of his bad behavior.

Remember that there is a difference between giving in and letting them manipulate you and you stepping in to correct what you know is not right or know is an inappropriate behavior. Monitor their activities with care and know when your toddler behaves in a negative way towards other children and intervene promptly. If they are in a group, take your toddler away for a little time to allow them to calm down. Learn to see what triggers their behavior as sometimes there are specific events or situations in which they become frustrated about something specific and throw a tantrum or fit.

The best way to avoid tantrums is to teach them positive-generating behaviors such as learning how to share by "taking turns" playing with a toy for example. You can do this yourself while playing with your toddler, and make sure you make it fun. Later when they play with other children they will be more prepared to play and share with others to minimize the possibilities of tantrums. Get in the habit of giving lots of praise and encourage them whenever they are doing the right things.

As a general rule, be patient whenever your toddler has a tantrum. Remove him or her from the location and try to calmly talk to him and see if he can begin to tell you what is bothering him. Be understanding and communicate it. If you exhaust your attempts just give him space as he will snap out of it. And remember it is more important to understand why they get tantrums in the first place, rather than trying to figure out all sorts of crazy ways on how to deal with them without understanding it first.

Chapter 18: Setting A Schedule For Your

Toddler

As important as it was for new parents to set a schedule for babies, it is equally important to keep, adjust this schedule for your toddler, so that you know exactly when to take up an activity. This helps in the smooth running of the home.

Here is looking at a simple planner to follow.

Feeding time

It will be important to feed your toddler at the correct time every day. Toddlers require nutrition in order to grow properly. It will be best to write down when you must feed your toddler so that you do so on time, every time, enforcing a schedule. Keep the healthy meals and snacks ready so that you can feed your child quickly if necessary. If you are a working parent and leave your child in the care of a caretaker, then give them proper instructions on what to feed your child and to feed them on time.

Training time

It is best to follow a schedule while training your toddler. Be it potty training, teaching them manners or taking up any such activity, you must set a specific time for the same and ensure that your toddler is ready to undergo the training. Don't be in a hurry to train them as it can get confusing and or overwhelming for them. Be patient and wait for your child to reciprocate your energy. With time, they will themselves be ready to take up a particular type of training without you having to tell them the same.

Playtime

Sketch out a separate playtime for your toddler. Doing so will help them develop a certain pattern. Set specific timings when your child has to take up an activity such as playing indoors with toys, going outdoors to play with friends etc.Playtime is an important part of life for your child, helping them develop motor skills etc. It is fine if they insist on playing for a longer time than that which you have set for them. Allow them to play to their heart's content as long as time permits.It helps them to sleep better at night.

Socialize

Set times for your toddler to socialize. It will be important for the toddler to meet new people and interact with them. Take your toddler out to play groups, parks and friend's places, so that your child meets as many new people and sees as many new faces as possible. Don't confine the child to the house, as a child can get very bored. Take your child to new places every week so that the child gets to have new experiences.

This is just a blueprint of the activities to take up and you can base yours on these.

Chapter 19: The Importance Of Good Nutrition: What Foods Should You Feed Your Child

I can tell you that you need to teach your kid a, b, c in order to improve their learning ability and nurture them to become smart children. However, when all is said and done, it all boils down to the kind of foods you feed your child. While the brain is naturally modified to learn new things at a fast pace, especially during childhood, you can boost your child's memorization skills at an early age by being selective of the kind of food they eat.

Common sense dictates that food is fuel, and is what makes the world of difference between waking up full of energy and in a sluggish mood. Generally, most experts will freely tell you that it is imperative to include omega 3 in your foods, for healthy brain development. On a typical scale, providing your child with the right kind of food can improve their concentration and mood in class. The reason why most nutritionists have been preaching about omega 3 fatty acids is their ability to enhance memory retention, mood and concentration. When taking omega 3, however, be cautious on the amount you feed your child. While it is true that omega 3 fatty acids play a major role in enhancing a child's memory, too much of it can lead to various complications. The best way to ensure your child has the right omega 3 provision is to strike a balance between their omega 6 and omega 3 concentration in the brain. Naturally, everyone's brain contains omega 3 fatty acids, but you need to compliment this with sources such as fish (salmon, herring and tuna), as well as omega 3 supplements such as fish oil. The recommended daily dosage of omega 3 for children is notably different from that of adults. In general, a normal adult should take about 3-4 grams of omega 3 fatty acids, while a child's daily omega 3 recommendation is about a third of the same. Some people prefer feeding their children with omega 3 supplements, rather than actual sources of the fats. Good examples of omega 3 fatty acid supplements include flax seed, wheat germ, omega 3 eggs, canola oil, walnuts, and fish oil. You can include about 1.5 to 2 grams of these in your child's meals everyday. However, most experts recommend that you distribute the grams among the child's three meals, rather than feeding them at once.

When packing your children's lunchboxes, try as much as possible to eliminate foods rich in fat. A good substitute for this is whole grains. These are rich in fiber, which makes the kids feel fuller for a long time. They also contain essentials nutrients and minerals such as potassium, magnesium and selenium. For example, for lunch you could pack turkey, hummus and pita chips.

This is a great afternoon brain booster. Turkey is a great source of protein that can provide your kid with the energy to concentrate in class. Hummus is rich in fat that can slow your child enough to focus in class. Pita chips, on the other hand, are a great source of carbohydrates that serve to fuel your kid's activities throughout the day. Another great lunch option is light chunk tuna, which is rich in essential amino acids that are required by your brain. Moreover, it is also a great source of omega 3 fatty acids needed for the overall function of the brain.

Similarly, you are also advised to pay close attention to the kind of snacks you provide for your children. Various snacks have different benefits in the body, and are required for different reasons. For instance, dark chocolate is a very rich source of important antioxidants known as flavanols, which play a major role in enhancing blood flow to the brain. It also contains sugar that acts as a source of fuel for the functioning of the brain. A little caffeine and various stimulants that boost cognition, mood and focus are also good for your child.

On the other hand, avocados also contain high levels of antioxidants that are great for the brain, just like omega 3 fatty acid foods. Generally, make sure that you eliminate as much as possible refined sugars and carbohydrates, and instead replace them with natural sugars such as maple syrup, fruit and honey, and whole grains. Foods rich in antioxidants also help to protect the brain from the effects of free radicals. Examples of foods rich in antioxidants include berries, red/green pepper, kiwis, avocadoes, red grapefruit, broccoli, Brussels, garlic and kale.

The next thing you need to keep in mind when preparing your kid's food is water. For decades, you have heard everyone emphasize on the importance of drinking water for your health. As such, the importance of water should not be underestimated when it comes to your child's well being. Water has several functions in the body. In fact, a lion's share of your body's fluid is water, which makes it a very important element of your health. Without water, your child's body will not be able to transport oxygen to and from various organs of the body. Moreover, failure to provide the body with the right amount of water can leave your child dehydrated. To ensure that your kid is well hydrated throughout the day, make a point of packing a bottle of water in his/her backpack every morning before they leave the house. In addition, let your child know of the importance of drinking water for his/her health to ensure that they are hydrated even when you are not around.

Apart from water, other drinks you can break the monotony with include fruit smoothies and energy drinks. The latter should be taken with caution as these usually contain caffeine that may should not be taken in large quantities as they may be harmful to your child. To be on the safe side, let them take these on an occasional basis, and not in the afternoon. Fruit smoothie ideas to use include making a blend of fruits that contain brain-building antioxidants and wheat germ or flax seed.

Effective Language & Communication

As your child grows, sooner or later, they will need to express themselves. Before a child learns to communicate, most of the cues you will receive from him/her are usually physical ones. Like crying when they are hungry, sick, or when they want to relieve themselves. Most kids start talking at around the age of two years. The process of learning language is quite a complex one. Your kid will usually learn how to talk through the words you converse with him/her. If you talk certain words repeatedly to them, the brain forms connections that enable your child to comprehend what you are saying. Talking to them often increases the number of words they can understand. You can improve the rate of learning for your child in various ways. A great way to go about this is to start reading to your child from an early age. The mirror game is also a practical method of teaching your toddler various parts of their body. You can take your child in front of the mirror and point out different parts of your body, saying them aloud as you indicate with your fingers. This will go a long way in making them aware of their body, and will allow them to learn that they are physically separate from the others, thereby enabling them to explore their own identity with language.

Talk with your toddler, even if the conversation will not be mutual. Take one of his/her toys and start talking about it playfully. To make the conversation interesting, add some cues like incorporating some actions while playing with your child's teddy bear. Teach them how to hug the toy as you do it yourself, and then take turns hugging the toy. Generally, the point here is to interact with your kid practically. While books and computers are essential in raising smartness in a child, your interactions with them are the ones that matter the most.

Chapter 20: How Divorce Affects Your

Children

You've likely spent months, or even years, agonizing over the decision to divorce. You may have chosen the path of divorce after finally rationalizing that it was the best course of action, but for your child, your divorce can come as a life-altering, painful shock. Every child is different, and the reaction to divorce tends to be a cyclical one, with children's behavior and feelings gradually altering over time.

Announcing the News

When you first announce the divorce, you should be prepared for anything. Some children may not fully comprehend the weight of this major decision; when you or your spouse move out, your children may have to be reminded that this is happening because of the divorce. This reaction is particularly common among young children, who don't have a strong concept of marriage and who may not understand that mommy and daddy can live separately.

In other cases, your child might actually be happy. Perhaps she sees the divorce as a way to alleviate the endless fighting between you and your spouse; or even as an opportunity for two birthdays or two Christmas'. Although she may seem happy now, it doesn't necessarily mean all is well. It can take several months for the true effects of divorce to creep in.

For other children, the reaction is swift and immediate. Your child might become angry and see your divorce as a betrayal, even as a sign you don't love her. She may be frightened or overwhelmed; worried about whether she'll be able to continue seeing both parents. Don't be surprised by tantrums, tears, or sullen silence. But no matter what your child's reaction is, don't judge her or discipline her for it. Your divorce is your creation, not your child's; she shouldn't have to suffer because your marriage is ending. Your primary job as a parent is to make the transition to divorced living a seamless one that minimizes your child's pain.

Reactions to the News

Researcher Elisabeth Kubler-Ross found that grief follows a predictable pattern, and your child's reaction to the divorce may neatly mimic this pattern.

First comes denial; your child may simply not believe the news, fail to comprehend how it will affect her, or simply ignore it altogether.

Shortly afterward, anger can creep in. This is when you might see tantrums, trouble at school, or an increase in sibling rivalry.

Bargaining is next. During this stage, children will do anything to reduce the pain they're in, and are more likely to blame themselves for the divorce. They believe that if they were nicer or better behaved, they could stop it all.

When bargaining doesn't work, depression can sneak in. Your child may become sullen, clingy, and spend much of her time crying, before the acceptance stage finally arrives.

Acceptance doesn't mean your child likes the divorce or experiences no side-effects. It simply means that she finally understands how it will affect her life and no longer tries to fight it.

Children can enter the stages of grief in any order, and may even repeat some stages. You must recognize which stage your child is in and allow them to experience it. Being supportive of how they are feeling plays a positive role in their overall development.

Life as a Child of Divorce

Research has consistently shown that divorce is harmful to children. However, this harm arises not from the divorce itself, but from how the parents manage their divorce. Custody disputes, bad mouthing your ex, trying to keep your child away from the other parent, and exposing your child to an endless stream of romantic interests, can extract a significant toll.

When divorce serves as a positive step toward minimizing conflict, and when it doesn't destroy a child's relationship with either of her parents, children tend to do much better. Despite your best efforts to protect her though, you can still expect some changes in your child.

Many children react to their parents' divorce by regressing. Young kids may "forget" their potty training or become afraid to sleep in their own rooms. Older children may become unusually needy or fearful. Regression is typically short-lived, particularly if you handle your divorce well. On the other hand, if your divorce grows nasty or contentious, or your child loses contact with her other parent, regression can last for months.

Behavioral problems are also common among children of divorce. Children often struggle to deal with challenging emotions. Rather than talking about their feelings, they're more likely to show you how they feel – with tantrums, trouble at school, fights with friends, talking back, or lying.

Research has shown that children of divorce are more likely to experience mental health problems such as depression and anxiety, even years after their parents' divorce. They have more trouble in school and are more likely to experiment with drugs, alcohol, and risky sexual behavior.

The effects of divorce don't end with childhood, either. A child's home environment is one of the most significant predictors of her social success. Children of divorced parents tend to have more trouble making friends, and this can extend to their romantic relationships as they reach adulthood. Adults whose parents were divorced are more likely to divorce themselves.

Children tend to bear the burden of divorce by going back and forth between their parents' houses, and having to explain to their friends when their parents are fighting.

Every measure of child welfare gets worse when the divorce is contentious. Children are more likely to suffer long-term effects when they feel caught in the middle, such as, having to listen to their parents insult one another, or having one parent abandon them.

You can't control everything about your divorce, but you can control your own behavior and shield your child from the worst effects of divorce. Doing so can make a big difference in her long-term well-being.

Chapter 21: A Physical Epidemic Among

Kids

There are many things to think about when becoming a single parent.And although many single parents are thrust into that role by an untimely death or the will of a partner, the majority of single parents are by choice.There are of course several parents who go into single parenting on their own.They either become mothers at a very young age and journey that long road or they determine later in life that they want a child.But whatever road has led to a single parent household, there is no getting away from the statistics that are attached to that road.Single parenting is a hard life, and it is even harder for the children or teens that are involved.And although kids are resilient, a lot of that is survival and they do survive, however, on the inside, and emotionally that is not always the case.

Of all the children born to married parents each year, fifty percent will experience the divorce of their parents before they reach their eighteenth birthday, and these statistics are expected to grow. Children that are a product of a divorced relationship experience many emotions and issues during the course of their life. And although not all kids experience the emotional perils of divorce, a large amount of them do, and suffer as a result. Of these children that are products of a broken home, sixty-five percent of them will experience divorce resulting in more emotionally erratic people.

Aside from the emotional and behavioral issues that occur among children of broken homes or single parent situations, statistics have shown that it actually affects the health of a child. Statistically, children of divorce are at a greater risk to experience injury, asthma, headaches and speech defects than those whose parents have remained married. And in addition to that statistic, children living with both parents are twenty to thirty-five percent more physically healthy than children from broken homes.

It is hard for many to want to link the two dynamics; however, it is a relatively simple concept. Children or teens of divorced families have a lot of anger, bitterness and frustration in their lives. Kids do not know how to process those emotions, and they should not be expected to understand such a dynamic, but like so many people that experience divorce, it is thrust upon them. The bitterness, anger and frustration manifest itself in the lives of these children and teens and because many times it is internalized, or they are unable to fully express or deal with it, it comes out physically. The emotional assaults on kid's lives as a result of a divorced home can deteriorate the child or teen physically. There is no magical formula for why that happens, just profound medical evidence that pent up hurt, anger and other negative emotions can take toll on a person's physical well-being.

Divorce hurts and it hurts everyone involved, but it especially takes a brutal toll on the product of the union, the children.The emotional and physical well-being of children's lives is radically altered as a result of single parenting through divorce.

Chapter 22: Child Support After Divorce

Child support is needed for the means of housing, transportation, food, clothing and providing the other necessities of life relative to the children. The amount of money that has to be paid out for child support is dependent upon many factors. If the ex-spouses can agree upon a set amount to be paid each outside the court system its less time consuming and complicated. It also eliminates the costly fees of paying an attorney, yet many are willing to go this route because they are not willing to pay a penny more then the court say they have to. The parent that has the children is the one that most likely will be receiving the child support payments. If there is equal sharing of the custody of the children then no child support maybe required. The payment of child support is based on the amount of money that each parent is making.If there are other children from another marriage then that has be calculated as well. The Specific laws of child will vary depending on the state that you live.Child support remains a bitter issue and often time affects the ex-spouses relationship long after the marriage has ended. In some case some individuals are so bitter that they refuse to pay court order child support in an effort to make it financially difficult for the ex-spouse to get by. Sometime it may be a matter of just not being able to afford to make the payments and make ends meet when there are lots of other bills involved.

Child support can be affected by job changed, being laid off medical problems etc; there is millions of dollars owed to recipients all over the world and the laws has imposed stiffer punishments for those who are not paying what the court system as deemed as fair.

For many divorced people, child support can be a financial burden.

Ex-Spouses New Partner Around The Children

After a divorce one or both spouses may begin to date other people and this sometimes spark jealousy as well as resentment because at some point this person will be in the presence of the children. Some divorcees just cannot accept someone else stepping into that role and being around their children even for a little while. This is something that divorced couples do end up dealing with though. Some divorcees will date casually while others will be more serious and eventually find someone to marry so your children will have a step parent in their lives. If a new marital partner comes into the mix then you will have to deal with it because you want to make sure the children are well taken care of. If you are confident that the ex-spouse is a good parent then your fears should be put to rest. It is highly unlikely the new spouse will treat the children unkind.

If hate and animosity is exhibited toward the new spouse then the children will surely pickup on it.They may be made to feel guilty if they have a likeness for the other person. It is important to discuss the new marital relationship issue openly with the children because they may have a hard time initially seeing their parent with someone new.Most children eventually adapt to divorce but some never give up the hope of their parents reuniting. Always impress upon children the need to have respect for the person the parent is dating or marries. They need to fell secure that these individuals do not replace their parents in any way. You should be prepared for the realization that the new spouse will be accompanying your ex-spouse to various events. Both ex-spouses should avoid discussing issues related to the marriage because this may cause negative perceptions.

When couples divorce sometimes love still lingers on; therefore, you should do your best to let go. You most likely will never become best friends with the new love in their life but it is to your advantage to get to know them on some level since they will be spending time with your children.

Chapter 23: The Need For Understanding

Nutritional Labels In A World Of Toxic

Ingredients

In a world of toxic ingredients in processed foods, including the threat of genetically modified foods, it is more important than ever to understand how to read nutritional and ingredient labels on the foods you purchase.And it is just as important to teach your children how to read these labels as well.When you bring food home, or even while you are grocery shopping with your child, show him/her what it is he/she should look for on a food label.In this way, the child will learn what is good to eat and what should be avoided.

When looking at a nutritional label, first look at the ingredients. Anything can be labeled as natural but still contain ingredients that are harmful to human health, so you want to verify that the product is, indeed, healthy and natural by checking what exactly is inside. You want to avoid any foods that use artificial preservatives, especially for possibly harmful preservatives such as BHT and BHA, as well as artificial dyes and flavors. Of course, anything artificial can lead to illness, so look for ingredients that are naturally preserved and flavored. If you cannot understand what an ingredient is because it has a chemical name, avoid it. And if you are looking to purchase organic foods, make sure to look for an official seal certifying that the food has been inspected and is, indeed, organic.

When looking at the rest of the nutritional label on a food, avoid anything that has trans fats, which are detrimental to health, and anything that is high in sugar and saturated fats as well. You want to eat foods that are fortified with vitamins and minerals and that are high in protein and healthy fats instead.

The more practice you get reading labels, the faster you will be able to do so at the store and the easier it will be for you.

Ways to Get Your Children to Choose Healthy Foods Instead of Junk Food

If children get hooked on fast food and junk food, it will make it harder for them to get used to eating healthier alternatives, so make sure you teach your children, from as early as when they are infants, to eat healthy fruits, vegetables, and grains that are loaded with vitamins, minerals, protein, and healthy fats. The only way to ensure that children will choose healthy foods over junk foods is to instill in them a love for the taste of healthy foods, along with an understanding of the negative health effects of fast food and junk foods, which are loaded with fats, sugars, and simple carbohydrates.

Junk foods and fast food can lead to many forms of disease, including obesity, diabetes, heart disease, and cancer. Even if your children are active, if they are not eating the proper diet, they will be at risk of acquiring these illnesses either when they are still young or later on in life, when their bodies simply will not be able to cope with the toxic burden these foods place upon them.
Teach your children the facts about the effects of food so that they can make the right decisions both in your presence as well as when you are not around to monitor their choices. In this way, you can rest assured that they will pass up the greasy burger and French fries for a healthier sandwich made with whole grains and fresh vegetables, and they will pass up the sugary snacks for healthier fruits, which are also sweet.

Traveling with Your Children to Stimulate Mental Growth

Traveling can be a fun activity for the entire family, and it can be especially beneficial for your children, who will get the opportunity to experience new sights, sounds, cultures, and foods. Traveling to various parts of your country and even trekking into other parts of the world will expose your children to mental stimulation and physical activity that will help them become well-rounded individuals who are true citizens of the world and have an appreciation for all races of people and their unique cultures.

In addition to seeing historical sites, taking in artwork, and exploring natural landscapes, from mountains to oceans, children who travel learn more through these experiences than they would in a classroom environment because they can experience everything in a hands-on way rather than merely having to imagine what these places and people are really like.

The best way to get your children to love traveling is to begin traveling with them once they are old enough to understand the journey they are on.Throughout the year, even during the school year, you can take them on short weekend trips or even daytrips to special spots that are located a relatively short distance from where you live.And during school breaks, especially summer vacation, you can really take advantage of the extra time off and take them to foreign countries or even exotic islands.It is a wonderful bonding experience for the entire family, and your children will have amazing stories to tell their friends when they return home.

Chapter 24: Coping When Things Go

Wrong

Suicide is never the answer. But when your teen is feeling overwhelmed by their emotions or all the things that are going on around them, they may feel like nothing is ever going to be better and that suicide is the only option that they have available to make it all work out. They may feel like they have no other choice, and that all their loved ones will do better without them. Once the suicide is complete, all that the family and loved ones are going to feel are sad and full of grief over this unexplained turn of events.

The only thing that you can do after the suicide is to take care of yourself. This is a horrible time for anyone, dealing with the death of their own child because of suicide. You need to be ready for some powerful emotions. This is not like the death of an elderly relative who has lived a full life and was ready to pass. This is your young child, someone who had a long life ahead of them and should have lived for many years after you passed away. This means that you will have a ton of emotions that are going through your head after this death.

Some of the emotions that you may feel when your loved one commits suicide include:

Shock—you are going to go through some disbelief and numbness of emotions when you experience someone committing suicide. You may not even believe that this suicide really happened.

Anger—some people feel anger that their loved one left them at all, or anger that they are left with all this grief. You could also feel some anger because you missed out on some of the clues that pointed to the suicide.

Guilt—you are going to feel guilty about the suicide, feeling like you should have done more to prevent it from happening.

Despair—you could feel helpless, lonely, and sad all at the same time. Some people will go through a physical collapse and even start to consider suicide themselves.

Confusion—figuring out why the suicide occurred and why your loved one resorted to this can make the time even harder.

Rejection—some wonder why their love or their relationship wasn't enough to help the loved one to stay around.

These emotions can stay around for a long time. Some people still feel them a number of months after the suicide happens. Consider getting yourself some help after the suicide to ensure that you are getting through this time and that you are not going to start having your own mental health issues at the same time.

Coping Strategies

The way that you deal with all of the grief that you are going through after the suicide of a loved one is going to make a difference in how well you recover and whether you need some assistance from a professional. There are a number of coping strategies that you can try out that will help you feel better, even though time is one of the best healers in this situation. Some of the coping strategies that you can try out include:

Keeping in touch—don't withdraw from those you are close to. Instead reach out to them and look for some comfort and some healing. You should have people who can be close to you, who will listen to your pain and help you get through this hard time.

Find your way of grieving—don't listen to what others say is the right way for grieving. You need to find your own method, rather than going for what others say is right. There is no right way of grieving, so find the way that works best for you.

Be ready for those hard reminders—they are going to come, no matter how much you would like to avoid them. Holidays, anniversaries, and other occasions are going to be painful during this time. You may need to consider suspending some of these activities for a short time until you are able to handle some of the grief.

Don't rush—when you lose someone you love to suicide, it is a hard thing to deal with. You need to heal at a pace that is right for you, so take your time. Don't let others tell you how quickly you should get through this process.

Expect some setbacks—there are going to be some days that are harder than others. You may think that things are going well, but then something hits you and the day goes bad. This is going to happen, so learn how to grieve in your own way and soon these setbacks won't be as hard to get over.

Consider a support group—there are often groups available in your area that can help you after a suicide. They will be full of others who have gone through the suicide as well. They can provide you with some more tips on how to get through this process so you can regain your life back again.

While there are a lot of coping techniques that you can try out in order to feel better after the suicide of a loved one, there are times when it can seem like too much. Consider finding a professional to help you get through these hard times if nothing seems to be working for you. They will be able to help you talk through the issue and will ensure that you are taking the best care of yourself possible. Don't try to go through this process on your own though; it is a hard process and everyone needs some help at one time or another so seek that help and learn how to cope after the loss of a loved one after suicide.

Chapter 25: Developmental

Considerations

As I stated earlier, it is important to think about the development of a child before you can determine what type of discipline to use with him. In this chapter, we are going to go over the developmental considerations that you need to think about when deciding what type of discipline you will use.

Birth to 12 months old:

Children this age are considered infants, and they need a schedule in order to regulate their functions and provide a sense of stability. They should be allowed to naturally learn how to deal with frustration as well as how to soothe themselves. Children of this age should not be disciplined until they are able to understand the difference between wrong and proper behavior. You should set an example for them, teach them wrong from right, but time-outs and other techniques should not be used at this age.

One year to two years old:

This is the stage when babies become toddlers, and it is important to understand that they will push limits, they will try to learn who is in control, and, if you do not take control at this time, you will have a very difficult few years ahead of you. You should be tolerant of the things your child does while he is trying to learn about the world around him, and you should be willing to teach him about the world around him.But you should also put limits on his behavior. Simply removing the child from the situation and telling him "No" firmly, while redirecting him, will work great.

You should never allow a child this age to be unsupervised.While you are observing the child, make sure you correct him when he displays improper behavior, to ensure that the behavior does not occur again. You have to make sure that you are not withholding your love from a child at any age, but especially at this age.

Children who are under the age of two are afraid of not being loved; they are afraid of being separated from their parents and so they should not be disciplined by being kept away from the parent. However, this does not mean that if you become frustrated and need time away from the child you are not allowed that.

You should not worry about giving the child this age an explanation as to why he cannot display a specific behavior, because he does not have the ability to understand what you are telling them.

Two years to three years old:

During this time in a child's life they will want to become masters of everything that they try, they will seek their independence while still wanting the parent close by, and they will begin to assert themselves.

The child may have outbursts because of becoming frustrated and not understanding why he is not able to do specific tasks. This should not be disciplined because he is not doing this out of defiance. Instead, you need to understand what is causing the outbursts and make sure that you are not expecting too much of the child too early. Make sure that as the parent you understand what the child is capable of doing and that you set limits for the child. You also need to make sure that the child is sticking to his routine – this will help you better understand if your child is getting upset.

When the child loses control of himself, you as the parent should be there to comfort him and then, as he calms down, you can reassure him that things are going to be okay. Redirect him to another activity and try to keep him away from the situation in the future. You will also want to give him a very short instruction on the behavior that you expect and why you expect that.

Three to five years old:

By the time a child is this age, he understands that there are limitations and expectations. He understands what behavior is acceptable and what is not, and he is able to provide many of his own needs. This does not mean that the rules you have set for him are nothing more than just words for him.Children this age are not able to make good decisions all of the time, and it is important that they have good examples to look up to as they learn how they should behave.

This is a time for you to remain consistent at all times; all of the rules should be enforced by all of the adults in the child's life. This is a time when you can begin setting rules and becoming more verbal with your child. You will still have to supervise the child and ensure that he is following directions.At this time you can begin using time-outs.

You should also provide praise for a child of this age when he has behaved well. Do not spend time lecturing a child this age – his attention span is not long enough for him to focus on what you are saying.

Six to twelve years old:

As a child grows he will want more independence, and this can lead to more conflicts. When a child begins school, he is often exposed for the first time to children that may or may not have been disciplined appropriately, and may or may not behave appropriately.

Children will begin choosing their activities and their friends, and they will begin to understand that there are other authorities besides their parents. This is a time for parents to observe their children, be a great role model for them, set the rules, and be consistent. This is also the time when they should allow the children to become more independent than before. Parents should make the big decisions – children of this age are not ready to handle those but they may be allowed to make the little decisions.

Praise children daily, but not excessively, in order to encourage the behavior that you want to see displayed and to discourage the behaviors that you do not want to see. The way that you discipline a child of this age may include taking away of privileges, grounding, and even time-outs.

Thirteen years to eighteen years old:

This is the time when most parents have conflicts with their children. This is because children of this age are becoming more independent – they are influenced by their peers and are beginning to challenge what they have been taught as they were growing up. They begin to understand that not everyone lives the same way that they do, and they begin to question their parent's knowledge.

Set rules in a way that does not make the child feel as if he is being set up for failure.

Do not belittle the child, and avoid long lectures. Let the child know that you understand what he is going through and that you are there for him. Do not spank a child of this age; instead choose a more appropriate discipline.

Remember that even though their attitude is changing and they are seeking their independence, teenagers still seek parental approval. Ensure that your child understands there are rules in place and there are consequences for breaking those rules, but do not argue with the child. Do not become confrontational with the child.

Chapter 26: Skin Protection With Kids

This seems like such a simple idea, but many parents forget to protect their children's skin when they are outside playing.I had a friend at the 4th of July parade that didn't bring sunblock or a hat for her child, and he had fair skin.Sun can not only damage their skin, but the sun can dehydrate a child and make them sick.There are some simple ways to protect your child from the sun.Product packaging has changes a lot in the last few years.You can now buy a bottle of sunblock that sprays directly onto the skin.You simply spray and rub.It makes less of a mess and is quick and easy to use.Whatever skin block you use, make sure to reapply if your child gets wet.

If you know your child will be outside during the day, you can help put on sunblock as they get dressed.They even have lotions that contain sunblock now.Don't forget their eyes.Little kids can wear sunglasses to protect their eyes from the sun.A hat will do the job also.Sun can reflect off of shiny surfaces and glare back at them.Keep their eyes protected. When the sun hides behind the clouds, don't think that your child will be okay in the sun without protection.If the cloud cover is thin, the harmful rays will still get through and can burn your child.Also, we tend to forget skin protection in the winter.If it's a sunny day with snow on the ground, the sun's rays will bounce off the snow and can burn your child's face.Skin protection is such an easy step to take now to help protect your child.Give them the extra protection that their skin needs.

Teaching Responsibility

It is so important to teach your kids responsibility, but many parents fail in this area.I watch parents that will not allow their children to do anything because they don't want to deal with the mess, they feel their child will fail, or they don't want to take the time.Yet, a responsible child needs these skills to be successful in school and to build a strong sense of self.There are many things you can do to teach your child responsibility.This is an important part of parenting.We will briefly discuss a few ideas.

Give your child chores or things around the house that they must do.Start a small child out by having them make their bed and put their toys away.Give older children jobs that must be done every day, or every week.Giving them work to do around the house helps them belong more to the family and the home. Find a pet that your child would like and help them learn to care for it.This teaches them to be responsible for another living thing.There are many different choices in pets and many pet stores will help you make that decision.

Make your child be responsible for the consequences of their actions.Allow them to make choices for themselves.Understanding that there are rewards and punishments for their actions helps to develop social skills they need. As our children grow, we can continue to provide opportunities where our children can learn and develop. Teaching responsibility now will help them make correct choices later in life. This is such an important skill to learn, and one that is easy to teach if we take the time.

How to Survive a Road Trip

Traveling by car with children can be a lot of fun, or a lot of frustration. Proper planning can make all the difference. Here are some tips to make your travel time a success. Print out a map showing the beginning and ending points, with larger cities marked. As you drive, have your kids mark off the cities or other landmarks on the map. This helps them see how far they have gone, how much farther you have to go, and teaches them about time and distance. It's also great to squash the "how much longer" questions.

Bring along games and books that they can play on their own, but also have some games you can play as a family.One of our favorites is to pick a topic, and then we rotate through the family.If we say "ice cream", then each person tells of a story or something they remember that involves ice cream.This is a great way to learn more about your children, as well as tell them some new stories. No road trip would be complete without snacks.Make a bag for each child with their own snacks inside.They can pick and choose what they would like, giving them some freedom and giving you a break.

Let them know beforehand that the treats must last through the whole trip so they won't eat them all at once.It's also fun to have some other treats stashed away that you can pull out when the kids are restless.A DVD player can be an easy way to entertain the kids while you are driving, but finding some family games and activities can help you bond with your children more and make the trip a better memory.If you have a DVD player in your car, don't rely on it for all the entertainment. Using the tips discussed here can make your trip easier, and bring you closer as a family.

Safety in the Home

When we bring a new baby home, most families prepare their house for the new arrival. As the child grows, safety measures are put into place, like locking cabinets and installing outlet covers. However, many families don't think about household safety as their kids get older. Here are some things to think about. Do you have an emergency plan in place for your children? Do they know where to go if you have to get out of the house quickly? Plan a location that is away from your house that can be a meeting place for all family members. Make sure your children understand the circumstances in which they would leave the house and wait at your meeting place.

Do your children know what to do if there is a fire in your house? Most parents figure that their children know to get out, but is it something that you have ever practiced?You only have a few minutes when the fire breaks out before all the oxygen is gone from the air and you need to have everyone out before then.Practice escape routes with your children. If there is an emergency in the home, do your kids know who to call?

Do they know how to dial 9-1-1?Can they tell their address to the operator on the phone?It is a good idea to have emergency information posted above the phone in your house.Write down the emergency numbers, and your address.Even adults have forgotten their address in a crisis. When you have an emergency, it is too late to plan.Make sure that you and your children have a plan in place to protect your family in an emergency.Don't wait until it's too late.

Chapter 27: Food For Thought

Kids should be shown how to feed themselves healthily from about the age of 10 or 11.A gradual increase in kitchen responsibilities should include being able to prepare a sandwich lunch, make toast, tea and coffee and clean up the kitchen counters and cabinets.By the time a teenager reaches the age of about 15 they should be able to cook a simple meal and know how to cook basic meat, chicken, fish, vegetables and snack foods.Not teaching these skills will lead to your kid being dependent on other people to eat one day – not good!

It is important to share kitchen chores.Single kids tend to have a greater understanding of the concept of sharing housework, probably as they have the advantage of one-to-one interaction with parents – households with more than one or even multiple kids must have a system of shared chores to be fair to everyone involved.Kids that take an active part in sharing chores at home as young teenagers are far better balanced in adult life so do not neglect this area of training for your kids.

Skills that help your child to survive alone and without your help are the most useful support line you can provide.We have children with one thought in our heads – to give them everything they need to excel – we then set about retarding every opportunity they have to be independent!If you are guilty of doing 'too much' for your teenager just stop it now – the biggest favour you can do your child is to teach him all he needs to know to go on without you -painful as it is!

While you are about the task of teaching Junior to cook, make sure you also teach him kitchen hygiene; how to shop; how to compare prices to get the best value; how to decipher nutrition information and how to balance meals so that he gets a healthy menu.The chances are he will sail off into the horizon and live on pizza for the next three years but when the time comes that he needs to be able to rustle up a meal or two he will remember what you taught him.If a third of what you imparted actually went in he will at least not poison himself or anyone else by eating six-day old chicken or mixing raw and cooked foods together in the refrigerator!

Letting Go

This is the worst part.You have spent nineteen years nurturing, teaching and cherishing and now he or she is leaving you.You have listened to all their troubles, nursed them when they were sick and lived through all their tantrums and tears. Forget how they will survive – how will you survive?What are you going to do with yourself now that your baby is leaving you alone?Who will you cook for and clean for?Who will you nag?Who will you shout at to pick up clothes from the floor or remember to shut off the lights?

Having to let go of a much loved child is like parting with half of yourself – and often it is the half you like the best! If you think your nineteen or twenty-year-old is a credit to you it is somehow of little comfort when you have to stand in a draughty bus station or rail terminus with a fixed concrete smile on your face, pretend you are ecstatically happy and proud and wave goodbye to the star of your universe. Most mums manage a dignified and matronly tear but no more – then confine themselves to bed for the rest of the day with a pseudo headache while they cry out their heartbreak.

Letting go hurts but let go you must if your child is to have a happy, healthy and well-balanced life. And of course there is the comfort of knowing it is not forever. Don't worry, they'll be back – usually when the latest love affair has turned sour or the laundry is out of control or when they need a cash loan from the Mum and Dad Bank.

Once big kids are grown there are a number of financial arrangements that rear their ugly heads, usually concerned with helping your kid 'get a start in life'.These cash outlays might be for a car; a wedding (which nowadays can cost a second mortgage); a deposit for a property or for costly business courses.

It is rarely a good idea to increase your own financial burdens to help out your children.And making a sweepingly generous gesture with one of your children could also mean offending younger siblings when it is their turn and there is no more cash in the coffers!Consider carefully before forking out a fortune to get the eldest daughter married off – you could end up seriously over-stretched and she might be divorced within two years!

Independence is an expensive business and your kids tend to learn how much they had at home when they have left for good.One lady with a delightful daughter who had moved into her own place arrived home from work one day to find the refrigerator was empty.Her daughter, having paid her share of the rent and bills found she was broke so went home and raided mother's pantry!!

Another woman whose spoiled son had moved into his own apartment a few miles down the road promptly turned herself into the unpaid housekeeper!She had her own key and would let herself into his apartment while he was at work each day.She then mopped, dusted and did his laundry before filling his fridge with all the nice little treats diddums loved and cooking a meal to be left for the little prince's return in the evening!

There comes a time when the apron strings have to be tearfully but firmly snipped forever.Don't you just love them though, those reassuring ties that hold your kids safe and secure till the end of time?Get a grip lady!Your kid is an adult and big enough to look after himself!

Empty Nest Syndrome

Any woman with grown up children will have felt that awful feeling of emptiness. It begins at the airport or the bus terminal or even on the front doorstep as you wave goodbye to the centre of your world as he or she wobbles off down the road with a bulging suitcase.

A lady with a houseful of screaming brats, toys scattered all over the floor and about four minutes spare in which to prepare the family dinner before heading back out to take Flossie to her music lesson will look forward to the time when the tribe is off her hands for good. The trouble is, when it gets here it's not as great as you thought it was going to be – at least not at first. You miss the sound of Smack Your Bitch Up at top volume rending the peace and quiet of a summer evening; the low-key teenage giggles that float on the air; the slamming doors and dirty socks on the stairs...

For women who become seriously ill as a result of ENS there is professional help which should begin with a visit to your doctor who will advise on the next steps to take.For those who go through a few days, weeks or even months of sadness but eventually emerge resolved to remodel their lives, there are loads of options.

'What you need is a hobby,' say your friends.But your hobby for most of the past twenty years has been closely linked with what the kids wanted to do, right?So here you are with all that energy you used to shape your children into the fine, upstanding human beings they have become and nothing to spend it on!

Don't worry. This time is in a way a period of mourning.The one thing that is not helpful is to cling to the son or daughter left behind, or keep hounding the one who just left when he or she is trying to make a life that is far removed from the one they had at home.You now need to have a new and different schedule and hopefully one that is as rewarding in its own way as the old one.

Chapter 28: Your Child Needs To Play And

Have A Hobby

At some point in your life you have heard someone say that's child's play, which probably made the activity at hand sound less than important. To our kids playing is and should be considered absolutely necessary for their overall development.

Most kids have plenty of energy to burn and playing can help reduce and harness all that excess energy. It also expands their motor skills while building the strength and stamina needed for their body to develop at a normal level. Our kids sensory learning is also enhanced through playing.

Our kids are natural curiosity seekers. Playing allows them to learn and understand most everything around them. As good parents we need to partner with our kids teachers to create and support the best learning environment possible.

There are many things and basic concepts about the world our kids would not know if they were not allowed to play. Every time they are playing they are learning to think on their own and solve the problems they can encounter. It sharpens their reasoning skills, learning how to count or build something by themselves.

If you think about it our kids learn to relate to each other when they are playing together. They quickly learn that sharing is something else they must do if they want to continue being included in group activities in order to be part of the team. Your child will also develop and keep new friends from playing with the group.

When your kids play with the group they fulfill some of the needs they have like receiving attention or that they accomplished something. Their self-esteem rises with a higher level of liking themselves for who they are. Much can be said for how they learn the proper ways to express the emotions they are feeling. They also learn how to deal with any fear or frustration they encounter.

As a good parent you must make it a point to encourage them to play. Get out the coloring books or the legos and create something together. Open up their imagination by constructing a tent out of a sheet or blanket and go camping with them. You must capture your time with them now because we all know how quickly time passes. Let them know that being a child is part of playing and they need to enjoy it now when they are one.

Your child needs to have a hobby as hobbies gives your kids the ability to express themselves and build their self-esteem at the same time. Hobbies are also a great way to help educate your children. Depending on the hobby they can learn more about astronomy or many other science subjects. Hobbies are another way of teaching your child to set and achieve goals. Don't forget about problem solving or makingdecisions. There are many talented individuals in the world that have turned their passions for a hobby into a great career.

As parents it is also a good thing to have hobbies of our own which sets a good example for our kids to do the same. Set aside a specific place where everyone can work on their hobby without any distractions. There are many hobbies that can cause a big mess so just be ready to accept this as a small price to pay for all the benefits received by your child.

Along with encouraging your kids to have a hobby it is also important to be there to provide general guidance and lots of support. Seize the opportunity to instill the right work ethics like listening and following directions. Demonstrate to them that anything worth having takes a lot of effort and work to get. Tell them it's alright to occasionally be frustrated when things don't go as smoothly as they hoped. Remind them that it is important to clean up their hobby mess when they are done.

This of course leaves them a clean area in which to work the next time they continue with their hobby activities.

By eliminating any distractions during hobby time your kids will receive the most benefit out of their hobby and learn that there is more to life than watching television, texting, or playing video games. We all know most kids spend way more time watching television than is spent in school or working at a great hobby. As a good parent you can set an example by not watching sports for hours or days on end. Work on your own hobby and you might just see an increase in side by side quality time with your child.

Having a hobby can be very rewarding and at the same time enrich many other areas of our lives. As a parent you owe it to yourself to encourage your kids to develop a hobby of their own that is in alignment with their interests.

Chapter 29: Parenting Plans

A divorce is a tough emotional time for most adults and it is often a time where people don't make the best decisions or act in the most adult and mature manner. Emotions are running high, people are feeling hurt, lost and sometimes betrayed and the future may not look very bright or rosy. Since this can be a turbulent time for parents, sitting down and taking the time to write out a plan for raising your kids that both parents will follow can really help parents start to co-parent and respect each others role in the emotional well being of the children.

Doing this plan on your own is the most collaborative way and the lowest cost way; however mediators, attorneys, parenting co-ordinators and family therapists can all be hired to assist the parents in writing a plan. In some cases a religious leader or family friend that both parents trust can act as an informal mediator or consultant to the co-parents.

WHAT IS A PARENTING PLAN?

In some areas a parenting plan is an actual component of the divorce and is filed with the court to show how both parents have agreed to parent the child or children. Even in areas where a parenting plan is not required by the court it is a still a working document that is a tool for parents to provide consistency, routine, security and stability for their child or children throughout the divorce and the years that follow.

A parenting plan can include be a simple handwritten document or it can also be one of several template type documents that are available for free over the internet. The more involved and detailed the parenting plan is the less room for misunderstanding or misinterpretation there will be with regards to the plan.

If the court in your location requires a parenting plan they will usually have a standard format that they use. For parents that are sitting down to complete a plan on their own for consistency in co-parenting, a simple bulleted list under the various headings or topics is often all that is required.

Conclusion

Thank you again for downloading this book!

As you see, parenting is one of the toughest jobs EVER!! However, with some good techniques and guidance on how parents should handle their children and situations well, rebellious or not. Therefore, both parents and children could have a more joyous and happy lives together.

I hope this book was able to help you to understand why some teenage children could be so uncontrollable and difficult to handle.

The next step is to know how to nor re-act but take a more pro-active part as a parent. LISTEN, to your child, most children that is ALL they really want. I realize we are busy and got a career, responsibilities and pressures outside of our families but we as parents need to prioritize our child first. I hope this book will help you and your child in ways to grow together and become happier family.

Thank you

www.ingramcontent.com/pod-product-compliance
Lightning Source LLC
Chambersburg PA
CBHW072004070526
44583CB00015B/1324